A NOTE TO PARENTS

Two characteristics of young children make their understanding of a miracle difficult. First, they are concrete in their thinking, and miracles are very abstract. Second, they do not have adequate past experience to recognize a miracle as something out of the ordinary. When they are hungry, it is as much a miracle that food is on the table as it is that Jesus fed a crowd. As far as numbers are concerned, a dozen holds the same significance as five thousand. It's simply a lot of people. Consequently, the main emphasis of miracles is that Jesus cared enough in these situations to do something to help people.

As you read this story, recall times that your child has been hungry or afraid, and assure the child that Jesus understands those needs and fears.

When you reach the conclusion, remind your child how nice it is to feel safe after you've been afraid. Point out that Jesus wanted his friends to be safe from the dangers of the rough sea.

— Delia Halverson

Delia Halverson is the consultant for *Family Time Bible Stories*. An interdenominational lecturer on religious education, she has written nine books, including *How Do Our Children Grow?*

Scripture sources: **Matthew 14:13-33, Mark 6:30-52, John 6:1-21**

FAMILY TIME
BIBLE
STORIES

THE MIRACLE OF THE LOAVES AND FISHES

Retold by Patricia T. Smith

Illustrated by Kirsten Soderlind

TIME LIFE Kids™

ALEXANDRIA, VIRGINIA

To Wayne —
Thanks for the boat!

truly,
Kirsten Soderlind

Jesus Christ lived long ago in a warm, dry country by the sea. He was many things: a teacher, a carpenter, and a caring leader for people who wanted to live a good life. Because he loved people, he performed miracles—amazing happenings that show people how God loves them and that help them believe in God. This story is about such miracles.

One day Jesus got into a boat and sailed across a wind-tossed sea. His friends, the disciples, went with him. When they reached the shore, Jesus stepped out of the swaying boat and faced a huge crowd of people. Many, many people had come to see Jesus—more than five thousand. Jesus moved among them for hours, healing the sick and speaking kind words.

Near the end of the day, the disciples said to Jesus, "It is growing late and the people are hungry. It is a long walk to the closest town or village. They should leave now to find food."

Jesus said, "The people do not need to go away. You can give them something to eat."

"But we have no food!" the disciples replied.

A little boy in the crowd
overheard Jesus and the disciples
talking. He tugged his mother's sleeve
and asked if they could share their bread
and fish with Jesus. His mother nodded.

"Now we have five loaves of bread and two fish that this boy shared with us," said Andrew, one of the disciples, "but that won't feed all of these people."

Jesus smiled. "Bring the food to me," he said.

Jesus thanked God for the food. Then he broke the bread and the fish into pieces and filled the disciples' baskets.

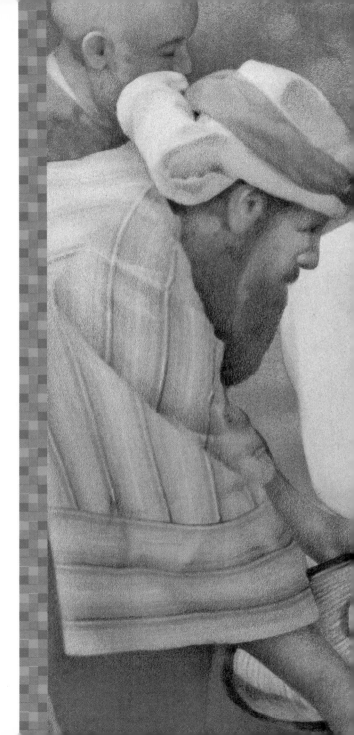

The disciples took the baskets of bread
and fish and walked into the crowd.

They gave the people all the food they
wanted to eat.

The boy enjoyed the bread and fish
with all the other people. As he was
eating, he felt a soft touch on his head.
He looked up and saw Jesus. Jesus
smiled at the boy and thanked him for
sharing his food.

No one who was with Jesus that
day went hungry. With just the five
loaves of bread and the two fish, Jesus
was able to feed the huge crowd of
people. There was even extra food. It
was a miracle.

It had been a long day.
Jesus wanted to be
alone to rest and pray.
He said good-bye to
his disciples and to the
crowd of people and
walked into the hills.

The disciples got into
their boat and began to
row home across the sea.
After a while, a storm
came. The wind blew
and the waves got bigger
and bigger. The tired
disciples kept rowing,
but they could not get
the boat to shore.

Jesus saw the storm and knew that his friends must need help. He came down from the hills and walked to them across the water, not sinking but stepping on the surface. The disciples were afraid when they saw someone walking toward them on top of the water.

But Jesus said to them, "It is I. Do not be afraid."

It was another miracle.

Jesus stepped into the boat with his friends. The wind stopped blowing and the sea was calm. Jesus and the disciples rowed safely home.

Time-Life Books is a division of Time-Life Inc.

TIME-LIFE INC.

PRESIDENT and CEO: George Artandi

TIME-LIFE BOOKS

PRESIDENT: John D. Hall
PUBLISHER/MANAGING EDITOR: Neil Kagan

FAMILY TIME BIBLE STORIES
THE MIRACLE OF THE LOAVES AND FISHES

Deputy Editor: Terrell D. Smith   *Produced by:*   Kirchoff/Wohlberg, Inc.
Director, New Product   Elizabeth D. Ward   866 United Nations Plaza
  Development: New York, NY 10017
Marketing Director: Wendy A. Foster
Marketing Manager: Janine Wilkin   *Series Director:*   Mary Jane Martin
Editorial Assistant: Mary Saxton   *Creative Director:*   Morris A. Kirchoff
Production Manager: Marlene Zack   *Design and Production:* Kelly Gabrysch
Quality Assurance Manager: Miriam P. Newton   Jessica A. Kirchoff
                                                                                David McCoy
                                                      Managing Editor: Nancy Pernick
                                                      Editor: Cynthia Rothman

First printing. Printed in U.S.A.   Published simultaneously in Canada.

School and library distribution by Time-Life Education,
P.O. Box 85026, Richmond, VA 23285-5026.
TIME-LIFE is a trademark of Time Warner Inc. U.S.A.
For subscription information, call 1-800-621-7026.

Library of Congress Cataloging-in-Publication Data

Smith, Patricia T.
The Miracle of the Loaves and Fishes / retold by Patricia T. Smith; illustrated by Kirsten Soderlind.
p. cm. — (Family time Bible stories) Summary: Tells about miracles performed by Jesus to show God's
love: the feeding of the five thousand, followed by Jesus walking on water.
ISBN 0-7835-4632-7
1. Jesus Christ—Miracles—Juvenile literature. [1. Jesus Christ—Miracles. 2. Bible stories—N.T.]
I. Soderlind, Kirsten, ill. II. Title. III. Series.
BT366.D36 1996   96-13150
226.7'09505— dc20   CIP
                                                     AC

For 500 Years
The Shackelford County Courthouse

For 500 Years

The Shackelford County Courthouse

by Shirley Caldwell, Bob Green and Reilly Nail

Introduction by A. C. Greene

1883

Bright Sky Press
Albany, Texas and New York, New York

Shackelford County Courthouse Restoration Committee

Ross Montgomery
County Judge and Committee Chairman

Mr. K.C. Jones

Mrs. Marcia Jacobs

Mr. Bob Davis

Mrs. Lynn Neff

Mr. Whitby George

Mrs. Dee Hamilton

Mrs. Diana Wilfong

Mr. Don Koch

Mr. and Mrs. Clifton Caldwell

Copyright © 2001 by Bright Sky Press
Manufactured in the United States of America
All rights reserved
First edition

Photographs courtesy The Old Jail Art Center,
Robert E. Nail Archives, pp. 8, 12, 17, 22, 27, 38–39,
44, 49, 54, 59, 66, 70, 80, 84, 88 and 98.
Photographs and architectural drawings courtesy
The Williams Company, AIA, pp. 3, 5, 7, 9, 101, 102,
107, 108, 111, 112, 114 and the Back Cover.
Photograph courtesy R. P. Mitchell pp. 32 and 64.
Photograph courtesy Betsy Parsons, p. 76.
Pen and ink drawing by Bill Cauble, p. 116.
Pencil drawing by Van Jones, p. 119.
Front Cover painting by Ronald Thomason,
courtesy of Molly Caldwell Cline.

The paper used in this book meets the minimum
requirements of the American National Standard for
Permanence of Paper for Printed Library Materials,
Z39.48-1984.

Designer: Donna Sicklesmith

Printed in the U.S.A. by Thomson-Shore, Inc.

ISBN 0-9709987-5-9

Preface

by **Ross Montgomery, County Judge**

THE CITIZENS OF OUR COUNTY have always taken pride in our history and through the *Fandangle* (a musical, historical drama) we have preserved that history. An appropriate quote from the *Fandangle* is "Over the trees and houses yonder, you folks can see the Courthouse Clock, ticking right up to the minute. Other counties may tear down their old Courthouses, replacing them with modern buildings of slick marble, mirrored glass and shiny chrome. But we in Albany cherish our Courthouse on its spacious square. We like timing our lives to the clock in its tower. You see, that clock counted hours for our fathers and our grandfathers and somehow as it measures our days, we are reminded of all the other lives it has ticked away. And that puts us in our place and that, to a great extent, we are what we are because of those who went before us across the prairie."

Our Courthouse being one of the oldest original Courthouses still in continued use is the pride and joy of Shackelford County. We had a wakeup call when the Hillsboro Courthouse burned. The people of our county rallied around the restoration program because we knew we could not take a chance on losing something that we all cherished. Our Courthouse is now not only the pride and joy of Shackelford County, but also the pride and joy of the State of Texas.

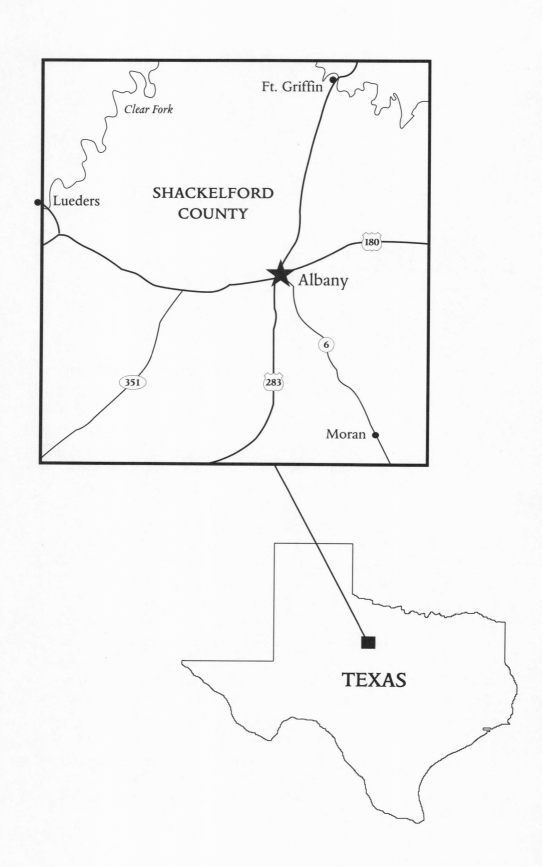

Contents

The Old Albany Courthouse

by A.C. Greene

SINCE BOYHOOD (and that's a tolerable length of time) the Shackelford County Courthouse in Albany has been part of my personal history and of my personal country, West Texas.

I was born in Abilene, and when I was five, maybe six years old, Congressman Thomas L. Blanton, from Albany ("The Watchdog of the Treasury"), built a big house on South Seventh Street in Abilene across the street from my parents. He planted saplings all along the front of his property and afternoons he was out watering them. I would cross South Seventh and trail around after him in his watering chores. Blanton, the politician, loved an audience, and a five-year-old who listened and apparently absorbed his philosophy was audience enough. And that was how I first heard of and was initiated into the mystique of Albany and its courthouse.

"The courthouse is the tallest thing in Albany and always will be," he declared. I applied my infant reasoning and asked, "What if they build a Wooten Hotel?" having in mind Abilene's new fourteen-story hostelry. "We'll just stretch the belfry," Congressman Blanton assured me. His tone on this, and most of his other declarations, rang out like bells. I asked my dad what a belfry was and when he told me I was puzzled as to how one stretched it but accepted the word of a Congressman, who ranked only a notch or two below my daddy and Brother Shepherd, our minister, in validity.

So, every time my family went traveling through Albany in our Model T or our Chevy touring car, I eagerly awaited the first view of the Albany courthouse. We crested Nine-mile hill, west of the town, curved along two wonderful loops of descending highway and there it was!

"The tallest thing in Albany!" I exclaimed the first time I saw it, adding, "always will be." My mother asked, "Who told you so?" "Congressman Blanton," I answered proudly, knowing she couldn't contest that.

And now, seventy years later, the Congressman's trees lap over South Seventh Street, the five-year-old has followed many politicians (none as convincing as Congressman Blanton), the wonderful loops on the highway have been eliminated (Alas!) but the Shackelford County Courthouse is still the tallest thing in Albany and, I hope, always will be.

The courthouse became a sign post on our journeys to Fort Worth and Dallas. "There it is!" someone would exclaim, proud to be the first to glimpse the shiny crest of the building—and adults were not immune to playing the game. Then in 1936 my father, Carl Greene, began to drive a delivery truck for the Pepsi-Cola Bottling Co. of Abilene. Pepsi was not as firmly established in West Texas then as it is now, so the weekly trip to serve the small towns was very important; besides, my father made two cents a case and if he sold the whole truck load of 200 cases, that meant four dollars which was not a bad sum per day in those Depression times.

We drove into Albany from the west and passed under a big sign that spanned the highway, "Albany Home of The Hereford." On the courthouse square was a huge iron kettle from the old salt works and all the buildings around the square had artistic nineteenth century facades which looked like a gunman might erupt shooting at any moment. After a few stops we proceeded on to Moran and across the dam to Cisco, and although the dam and "the world's largest outdoor swimming pool" were exciting, they weren't historic—and the Albany courthouse was, and I was already judging everything by its historic value.

Then in 1957 when, as a reporter, I was in Albany to write half a dozen stories a year, the late Robert Nail showed me a blueprint of the courthouse designed by J. E. Flanders and offered to take me to the very top. Up we went, climbing to where the clock is and Bob said, "This next part is scary." We clambered over the copper roofing toward the bell tower and just as we reached it, the big bell began to bong, right in my ear, and it was so sudden and unexpected I almost jumped from the tower. In 1964 when I spent three weeks in his home across the street from the courthouse, the deep bell became a reassuring night watchman, saying, "All's Well!"

The courthouse became "Albany!" to me, and I attended a dozen *Fandangles* when the spotlight shown on the old tower in the distance, sending a shiver of history down my back.

The prime moment for the Shackelford County Courthouse and me was on January 19, 1990, when Judy Dalton Hyland, who had never been in it, and I went in to the county clerk's office and applied for a marriage license. Everything was ready: the clerk stopped her typing at one point to tell us, "I'm more nervous than you are!" By the time the application was finished and signed it seemed like half of Albany had either heard we were in the courthouse or were sending everything from flowers to candy to us and posing us on the western entrance of the grand old building. Nancy Green had smoothed the legal road for us, getting everything ready (including a minister) and preparing a wedding supper. Both were used the next night, January 20, 1990, at our wedding in front of the big fireplace at the Bob Green Ranch, with the minister wearing cowboy boots and more than fifty guests who showed up for our "simple" ceremony. The girl from Missouri at my side still can't get over how easily we were welcomed into the Shackelford County family.

Today we have our Shackelford County marriage license hanging just below a Hereford hide Bob Green gave us as a wedding present.

Do you wonder why the Albany courthouse is a sacred shrine to A. C. and Judy Greene?

11

CIRCA 1890

1

A History of the
Shackelford County Courthouse

by Shirley Caldwell

FOR 117 YEARS the bold relief on the facade of the Shackelford County Courthouse has wrapped itself around the very heartbeat of all of us living here. As a vital part of modern life it links us to a frontier past as colorful as any in the Old West. Overlooking our lives, the magnificent structure, hand-carved from native limestone, of three stories and topped with bell and clock tower, is symbolic of who we are and the journey we've made. Simply said, it tells our story.

Just sixteen miles north of the courthouse, a thin band of water winds through the dry prairie. This river is responsible for early Native American presence and later pioneer settlement in this part of Texas. A scarcity of fresh water in west Central Texas brought people to the banks of the Clear Fork of the Brazos River and it transects Shackelford County's northern boundary. The North Prong of Hubbard Creek and smaller sources such as Deep Creek also water "the dry and dusty plain" of the county, but it is the Clear Fork that was central to the western frontier history of Texas.

In 1849, while laying out a road from Dona Ana, New Mexico, to Fort Smith, Arkansas, for the United States Army, Captain Randolph B. Marcy passed just to the north of our Clear Fork area. He came back to the Clear Fork in 1851 because it had impressed him with so much potential for a military post. The result of this visit was Fort Phantom Hill, founded by the Fifth U. S. Infantry with Major J. J. Abercrombie in command. This fort was poorly located for good water and a supply of trees for lumber. It was abandoned after three years but served unofficial purposes until the last quarter of the century.

Marcy returned with Robert S. Neighbors, representative of the Indian Department, to explore further in 1854 and to locate the Comanche Indian Reservation in what is now southwestern Throckmorton County near the road from Fort Belknap to Fort Phantom Hill. This time they visited the farm of U. S. Indian Agent Jesse Stem and selected a nearby site for the reservation that was close to the river. The courageous Jesse Stem of Ohio holds the distinction of being the first white man to settle along the Clear Fork and did so at the behest of the U. S. Government as an Indian Agent appointed by President Rutherford B. Hayes. He arrived unarmed to an area on the river considered a favorite Comanche camping grounds, and true to his Midwestern upbringing the provident Stem set up his Agency for the Indians of Texas and began to raise grain and livestock. The nearest armed troops were thirty miles away.

A year later in his report to the government Marcy recommended that a fort be located on the Clear Fork. It would be accomplished too late to protect Stem who was clubbed to death by two Kickapoo Indians as he returned to Fort Belknap.

As a result of Marcy's survey, Camp Cooper was established by Major W. I. Hardee on the river near the reservation on January 2, 1856, seven miles north from the present site of Fort Griffin. Two years later Shackelford County was created by the Texas Legislature and named for Dr. Jack Shackelford from Alabama, physician hero of the Texas Revolution who was spared at Goliad.

Under the protection of the U. S. Army at Camp Cooper with Lieutenant Colonel Robert E. Lee in command, settlers made their way to the Clear Fork. The army sent its best to train on the frontier of Texas. The following is a list of military men, probably incomplete, in addition to Lee, who prior to the Civil War spent time at Camp Cooper or passed through the camp on their way to search for Indians: George Thomas, William Hardee, Earl Van Dorn, E. Kirby Smith, George Stoneman, Jr., John B. Hood, Theodore O'Hara, Charles J. Whiting, Innis N. Palmer, Kenner Garrard, Fitzhugh Lee, Nathan "Shanks" Evans, William B. Royall, William W. Lowe, John W. Spangler, Richard W. Johnson, Robert Hall Chilton, and Lawrence Sullivan "Sul" Ross who later became Governor of Texas. Searching for Indians out of Camp Cooper provided experience in guerrilla warfare, and these men went on to serve for either the Union or the Confederacy, and several became famous for their exploits.

One of the most famous Texas personages to visit Cooper was Cynthia Ann Parker. In 1860, she was found during a battle on Mule Creek on the Pease

River, betrayed to the soldiers by her blue eyes. She had been captured as a child by the Comanches from her family's fort and had grown up with the tribe and married Chief Peta Nocona. They had three children—two boys, Quanah and Pecos, and Topsannah, a girl who was with her mother when captured. In taking Cynthia Ann back to civilization, Sul Ross stopped at Camp Cooper, but she never could adjust to the white man's way of life, and her little girl died soon after they were found. Quanah Parker became the last great chief of the Comanche Nation.

Although abandoned as a federal post when the Civil War started, Camp Cooper became a supply point used for provisions and ammunition by Colonel Buck Barry and Companies C and H of the Texas Mounted Rifles of the Frontier Regiment, forerunner of the Texas Rangers. Camp Cooper served sporadically for bivouacs until 1872. In 1867 after the war, Fort Griffin was established, and the settlement which had come to a halt during the four-year conflict continued. There were settlers in other sections of the area as well.

They came to the southeast corner and settled on Deep Creek in the early 1860s. During the war they built a temporary family fort on the creek called Mugginsville. George Greer, a devout southerner from Tennessee, came to about six miles north of the present town of Moran in 1860. Greer and his wife, Sarah, built a rock house that they used as an early stagecoach stop. Joseph Beck Matthews arrived with his family from Louisiana in 1859, along with the family of Barber Watkins Reynolds from Alabama. They moved to the northwestern part of the county area right on the Clear Fork and into what was later Throckmorton County. J. C. and Fannie Lynch came in 1858, back to the country they had spotted near the middle of the county while on their way to California and the gold rush, and the W. H. Ledbetter family came from Georgia and reached the Clear Fork in 1859. It was 174 of these early pioneers, these same adventurous and sturdy souls, who in August 1874 organized Shackelford County. A month later they convened the first county court at Fort Griffin in the law office of Stribling and Kirkland.

Cornelius Kincheloe Stribling, a native of Alabama, was chosen as the first presiding judge of the Shackelford County Court. He came to Texas in 1841 at the age of eight. He was later admitted to the bar in San Antonio and served in the Civil War with Terry's Texas Rangers. He and his wife chose the outermost part of the frontier as their home after the war partly because T. E. Jackson, a friend, had a store in Fort Griffin. Another acquaintance was J. C. Lynch who urged Stribling to give up his law practice at Palo Pinto with William G. Veal and move to Fort Griffin to become the first cattle inspector in that area. This position was meant to curb cattle rustling. Stribling was a leader and later served two terms in the Texas Legislature. His partner, George A. "Kirk" Kirkland of South

15

Carolina, was appointed first county surveyor. Four years after Shackelford County organized, Kirkland moved to the new Taylor County, opened an office at Buffalo Gap, and later became a prominent lawyer and leading citizen of Abilene.

It is true that the first officers of the court were southerners, however, Fort Griffin had a mixture of geographical representation among its citizenry as our story will reveal.

Stribling's office served as "voting poll" of Precinct No. 1 as well as location of the court. W. H. Ledbetter eventually established a salt works on the Salt Prong of Hubbard Creek twenty miles south. He served as Precinct Justice No. 2. Originally from Alabama, Joseph Beck Matthews, a rancher, acted as Precinct Justice No. 3. J. S. Steel was Justice for Precinct No. 4, and John C. Lynch, rancher and a native of Ireland, was Justice of Precinct No. 5. Selected as county clerk was P. J. Clark, and Henry C. Jacobs from Kentucky served as sheriff. The homes of the justices were used for voting places.

There is undeniable evidence that the town of Fort Griffin became a rough place as it grew up on the river flat at the bottom of the fort's hill. A number of old timers left behind excellent memoirs that unanimously testify to this, and circumstances bear out their memories. An excellently researched book, *A Texas Frontier*, written in 1996 by Ty Cashion, attempts to revise the violent emphasis of Fort Griffin's history and succeeds in presenting plausible arguments; however, even he makes this concession, "Make no mistake about it: by frontier standards this was a violent place."

Starting in 1874 hundreds of thousands of longhorn cattle and horses from South Texas were driven to Kansas and Nebraska over the Western Cattle Trail, sometimes called the Dodge City Trail. Trail drivers and cowboys stopped to quench their thirst at the "Flat." Griffin became a main supply point on the trail. Drovers and drifters could enjoy the company of some of the local ladies such as Sally Watson, Indian Kate, Nancy Sharpe, Long Kate, or Sway-Backed Mag at one of the town's saloons. Some of the west's most notorious names were drawn into the swirl at Griffin—Doc Holiday, Wyatt Earp, Big Nose Kate, Hurricane Bill and his girlfriend, Hurricane Minnie.

Prostitution and gambling were routinely tolerated, though local law officials tried to slow the obvious and varied recreation for which Griffin became known by regularly taking offenders to court and issuing fines. In spite of this, one could gamble with the mysterious Lottie Deno (Charlotte Tompkins) in the back room of the Bee Hive Saloon or visit Mollie McCabe's "Place of Beautiful Sin." Thrust into this cultural mix had been added the remainder of the Tonkawa Indian tribe who lived nearby Fort Griffin in order to receive the army's protection.

Added to such a fascinating blend of humanity were the hunters commonly slaughtering buffalo on the prairie west of Griffin. They brought their hides in

16

1883

17

for shipment to what quickly became a sizable town. The newspaper of the day, *The Frontier Echo* in Jacksboro, commented on the "high smell" of the hide stacks awaiting shipment on wagons rolling east and north from Griffin. At the height of the hunting, buffalo stacks would cover several acres at a time and number in the thousands.

Of course, the soldiers at the fort added another volatile dimension. From 1869 to 1874 companies of the African-American Twenty-fourth Infantry and the Ninth Infantry, now popularly called Buffalo Soldiers, were stationed there along with companies of white soldiers. Race relations not being what they are now, fracases did occur and some involved civilians, but they were rare, Cashion says.

A little earlier, the fort was used as a supply base for soldiers traveling the Mackenzie Trail to take part in the Red River Indian Wars. Named for General Ranald S. Mackenzie, a New York native and also a Union officer, the trail was followed later by settlers heading northwest to new Texas land available because Native Americans had been removed to reservations. Mackenzie himself organized troops at the old Camp Cooper site in 1871–72.

Such disparate intermingling of mankind required some attempt to establish rules of conduct apart from the military presence. Primarily law enforcement remained a local concern handled by local people. Little official influence other than soldiers at the fort found its way to this isolated area except during the vigilante period. Rangers or the U. S. Cavalry could only travel "40 miles a day on beans and hay" on an average day.

During the Civil War, a group of men secretly sought to maintain law and order in Parker County and in the Palo Pinto area, then called Golconda, by punishing the guilty without due process, most times with the swift justice of a tree and a rope. The Old Law Mob, as they were called, took credit for several hangings. This influence was felt in the Clear Fork country. After the war, during the 1870s, a similar group operated in the Fort Griffin area called the Tin Hat Band Brigade or the Vigilance Committee. They tagged their victims with signs that said "Horse Thief No. 1" and "Horse Thief No. 2" as they hung from tree limbs to warn others who might be tempted.

Aunt Hank Smith came to Fort Griffin in 1873 and commented on the organization in her memoirs written in 1924: "The better citizens of the town organized a vigilance committee who generally did the hanging." This type of activity was by no means unique to this area of the state although Fort Griffin's Committee was very active in attempting to rid itself of horse thieves and cattle rustlers.

Edgar Rye states the following about the vigilantes in *The Quirt and The Spur*, his autobiography written as a novel in 1909. Rye had arrived at Fort Griffin from Kentucky in 1876 at the age of twenty-eight:

> When it is understood that the honest, legitimate citizens were in the minority and scattered over a large area, while thieves, robbers and murderers were banded together and did not hesitate to testify falsely in court or waylay and kill witnesses to prevent conviction, the necessity to organize a Vigilance Committee to rid the community of these lawless characters when the law was impotent, at once becomes apparent.

Other men and women of that era left similar comments concerning the nature of the organization. It is easy from the vantage point of 125 years to criticize the cruel activities of the vigilantes, but we must consider in either condoning or condemning that these were desperate times and most of those involved were desperately taking a course of action out of fear for their livelihood and their families. Not only do we now see these actions as blatantly illegal, but we do not understand the serious dilemmas leveled when stealing one's horse or cattle. We have the luxury of only seeing these events in a historical context with the protection of never having experienced such obstacles and threats in our lives.

Recent historical writers have speculated that Rye himself was a vigilante. Perhaps, perhaps not. Ranger Captain Arrington wrote to Major John B. Jones, "I am satisfied that at one time nearly everybody belonged to the mob." Rye was in a position to know firsthand all of the parties, having served as a county precinct justice, lawyer, county attorney, and newspaper editor.

Editor of the *Fort Griffin Echo* was G. W. Robson, a Union officer from the Midwest who edited a paper called *The Frontier Echo* in Jacksboro, then Fort Griffin and finally Albany. He made frequent mention of the committee's work in his paper, referring to the hangings they conducted as "house cleaning." These two men, but principally Rye, were to play a role in the building of the Shackelford County Courthouse by using their influence as journalists.

When the second county court meeting took place, Henry Jacobs opened the court proceeding by reading a proclamation from "His Excellancy Richard Coke, Governor of Texas, dated October 12, ordering an election to locate permanently the county seat . . . and to locate temporarily the county seat . . . within 1 mile of Fort Griffin at such place as the county court may direct until said election." The county's founding fathers were a more homogeneous group than Fort Griffin's inhabitants and certainly more determined to bring stability and respectability to the Clear Fork area. In furthering their aspirations for an orderly and lawful society, Henry Jacobs, sheriff of the new county, promoted for county seat an unsettled area that he was in the process of acquiring nearer the center of the county, sixteen miles south of Griffin.

On November 8, 1874, an election determined the permanent county seat to be the Northeast Quarter of Section #1 of the Blind Asylum Survey on the North Prong of Hubbard Creek over Fort Griffin, 54 to 39. This was the land that Jacobs had promoted. So, in January, he generously offered a welcome commodity. He gave land with the provision that a courthouse be built within a year. The gift included the spacious lot, 420 x 420, for a public square, courthouse, and other public buildings and land for broad streets and alleys. Further, he gave additional land to benefit empty county coffers—one-half of eighty-eight business lots and seventy-six residence lots in the still unnamed county seat.

By May, the court accepted William Downtain's proposal of $800 for building a courthouse. The court minutes reveal a summary description of the courthouse as follows. It was to be:

> One story high, 45 x 20 ft. with six windows in the side, a folding
> door in the west end, be 8 ft. from floor to ceiling, covered with
> cypress shingles, have pine floors, 5 ft. paneled doors with good lock
> and key, opening windows with 12 lights 10 x 12 in. with sash and
> glass, two of which have outside shutters, divided into two rooms by
> a wooden partition 10 x 15 ft. off the east end, made of cedar pickets
> set in ground or on sills of a stone wall 18 in. thick, and have hewed
> post oak window sills.

19

In July, the county seat was named "Albany" by then Deputy Sheriff William R. "Bill" Cruger for his hometown of Albany, Georgia, with the stipulation that Henry Jacobs would have the option of selecting another name if Albany had been taken. Jacobs rightfully deserves the title "Father of Albany."

Henry Herron was a native of Wisconsin who at the age of twenty came to Griffin in 1875. Herron's family ran a boarding house just off the square behind the old Castleberry Furniture Store (now the Dollar Store) called the Herron House. In his memoirs taken by J. R. Webb of Albany, Herron tells that the first person living in the new town was T. H. Barre who had a dugout and a tent for a residence on the lot where the Nail House now stands. Barre later gave land for the cemetery and was a county commissioner when the stone courthouse was built. John Jacobs, a buffalo hunter and brother of Henry, built a one-room picket home from post oaks imported from Stephens County. The John Jacobs' had Albany's first baby, a boy named Albert. The first permanent structure to be built, however, was the modest stone house of Henry Jacobs.

As soon as the two-room picket courthouse occupied a very small spot on the large public meadow, the county clerk was instructed to move the records to Albany. The court ordered two tables and four benches made and a stove and pipe be installed. Jacobs' stipulation of a courthouse within a year had been met. By all signs construction was a rushed-up job because almost immediately the county had trouble with the building. Four months after the job was deemed finished, Jacobs was paid "$3.50 for propping the west end of the court house."

Mr. Herron tells of seeing three men gathered around the picket courthouse. Herron stopped by to see what was going on and saw two tough-looking men handcuffed together, sitting on a bedroll inside. Asking one of the men outside who they were, he was told, "A couple of horse thieves." The very next morning the two were found "hanging to an elm tree in a grove just west of where the Jim George residence now stands." At Jacksboro *The Frontier Echo* reported that fifty men of the "Hanging Committee" had taken part in the punishment of Bill Henderson and Hank Floyd on June 2, 1876. Other reports said fifty men were on foot and twenty on horseback.

Being unable to pay Downtain in full for the courthouse, the county officials wasted no time in selling off some lots. Two women, Susannah Gunsolus and her sister Fannie (Mrs. J. C.) Lynch, purchased the first commercial lots.

Meanwhile, the county needed roads. They were graded as a "First Clop" or a "Second Clop" road. The process of making these new roads "clopified" had to have been an attempt at making the surface hard and somewhat weatherproof. Roads were built to link Albany to Fort Griffin and to the Greer Ranch south of Albany, and regular mail delivery was increased to six times a week from Albany to Fort Griffin.

20

Hank Smith, a native German, was awarded an exclusive privilege to operate a ferry across the Clear Fork at Fort Griffin. His fee schedule charged twenty-five cents for a person on foot, one dollar for buggies, carriages, hacks, and two horse wagons, and fifty cents for a man and horse or a man and mule. Uncle Hank, as he was called, had a diplomatic personality, especially in dealing with drunks, and he spoke English, German, Spanish, and four Indian languages. He built and for a while ran the two-storied Occidental Hotel in Griffin where his wife, Aunt Hank, cooked. Elizabeth Boyle Smith had emigrated from Scotland with her four brothers and settled at Fort Griffin where she met and married Hank. It was said that every state in the union and several countries were represented at Griffin.

In 1876, elections were held. W. H. Ledbetter won as county judge and John M. Larn as sheriff and collector of state and county taxes. Larn was a native of Alabama who had come to Griffin by way of Colorado. Little accurate history is known about him. He is said to have been charming and polite to ladies, and he married Mary Matthews, daughter of J. B. Matthews, one of the founding officers of the county. People who knew him said Larn had "a strong and pleasant personality—a typical cowboy." Residents of the "Flat" backed Larn over Sheriff Henry Jacobs, which is understandable. After all, Jacobs had promoted Albany over Fort Griffin as county seat. For a while Larn was a good sheriff who pleased all factions. His close friend, neighbor, and business partner was John Selman who had come to Griffin from Fort Davis, the family fort in Stephens County. Selman lived there with his mother after having deserted from the Confederate Army during the Civil War. In spite of Larn's likable personality, it was not long before Larn's good reputation became suspect.

In the first two years of county life, official business must have been fairly time-consuming because a number of counties surrounding Shackelford County were attached to it for voting and judicial purposes including Taylor, Callahan, Throckmorton, Haskell, Stephens, and Jones counties. It was agreed that Judge Ledbetter be paid a salary of $250 a year and that was quickly changed to $360.

Despite the county sustaining heavy expenses for transporting prisoners and handling the heavy docket of lawless activity, Sheriff Larn did not attend court regularly so Bill Cruger served as acting sheriff. In fact, less than a year into his term, Larn resigned from his office, reportedly because he did not get along with Cruger who had killed Billy Bland, one of Larn's friends, in a shoot-out at the Bee Hive Saloon in Griffin. Cruger resigned as assessor of the county taxes and was appointed sheriff. Exactly one day before his resignation in March 1877, Larn was ordered by the court to pay $155.39 "for the amount due County of Jones for non-resident taxes to Aug. 31, 1876." At the same time, Larn was reimbursed for $27.50 to cover the purchase of two sets of handcuffs and shackles for the county.

The first time Larn came under scrutiny occurred at Fort Griffin where he was questioned and released. Evidently, his reputation had so rapidly deteriorated that on June 21, 1878, Edgar Rye, acting as Justice of the Peace for Precinct No. 1, had the sheriff issue a warrant for John Selman, John M. Larn, Thomas Curtis, John Gross, Thomas Selman, and Thistle and Jimmy Herrington of Throckmorton County, to appear in Albany at the courthouse and answer charges filed by A. T. Lancaster and William Brisky. These two men had been threatened with bodily harm by the six men led by Larn. Then, just over a year after resigning as sheriff, Larn was arrested again, this time by Sheriff Cruger and a posse at Larn's Camp Cooper Ranch. He was taken unarmed by surprise one morning as he came out to do milking chores. This time he was taken to Albany where Herron, as part of his deputy job, took him to have the shackles riveted on his legs, a set Larn may have purchased himself. Mrs. Larn hired J. W. Wray, a lawyer at Griffin, and followed them to Albany, renting a room at the hotel.

Thus, while he was shackled in the temporary jail in Albany, the so-called mob of vigilantes broke into the jail, surrounding John William Poe and Henry Cruger, the guards on duty. At the same time they overpowered and disarmed Ed Merritt and Robert Slack, two other guards who were asleep, and woke up Larn. By eyewitness accounts given a few hours later, Larn was then shot to death by

1884

22

some members of the mob. It is possible that Mary heard the shots from her hotel room.

In the inquisition of the four witnesses, some facts were agreed upon and some were not. The estimate of men in the mob ranged from twenty to thirty-five, the time of the attack was agreed at between midnight and 1:00 A.M. on the morning of June 24, all said the vigilantes were on foot and left heading south. No one recognized any of them because they were all masked. According to these same four eyewitnesses, Larn said nothing and neither did the shooters except for one who from the outside cautioned "That's enough" or something to that effect. There was confusion on how many men did the shooting and how many shots were fired. Poe said that he went immediately for help upon seeing Larn's body and brought E. R. Manning to the guardhouse. Edgar Rye, Justice of the Peace, signed the inquest along with six of Albany's prominent citizens— T. H. Barre, J. M. Herron, E. R. Manning, Henry Palm, Charles Reinbold, and N. H. Miller. It was sworn that there were nine pistol shots to the body as the cause of death.

This official account differs from Rye's version in his 1909 book. According to Rye eleven men stepped up and shot the one-time sheriff to death at close range with their rifles and only after an elaborate dialogue was exchanged between the parties. This was a version repeated by Sophie Poe in her book *Buckboard Days*, written in 1936, after her husband's death. Rye wrote his account thirty-one years after the incident. Perhaps his memory allowed for some "poetic license." Nevertheless, before Selman could lead their gang, named in the warrant, from the "Flat" to Albany in a rescue effort, Larn was dead.

Larn lived in a beautiful rock house he built on his Clear Fork Ranch from where he had been supplying beef to the soldiers and the Tonkawa Indians. Allegedly, according to oral accounts, cattle hides were recovered from a big hole of water near his house, proving that he had rustled cattle and altered brands in order to meet the three beefs a day he was to furnish the fort. After his death, his wife Mary took his body to their ranch and buried him behind their home. The newspapers of this area carried sensational accounts of Larn's arrest and subsequent murder. The *Fort Worth Daily Democrat* quoted Deputy Sheriff W. O. Beach of Palo Pinto who reported from Breckenridge that one member of the mob beckoned to another who stepped forward and shot Larn in the forehead before others fired into his body. According to this account, the vigilantes wore handkerchiefs over their faces and long slickers. All the same, there is credible proof that Larn knew most of the men who killed him.

Two Matthews descendants who understood the value of history—Joe Blanton assisted by his uncle Watt Matthews—in an effort to set the record straight wrote a small book shortly before their deaths entitled *John Larn* in which they tell this story from the Mary Larn family perspective. Watt was a nephew of Mary but was born twenty-one years after the death of the infamous sheriff. Their sincere attempt to record the story as they had heard it possibly came in response to two recent books, the already mentioned Cashion book and *The Frontier World of Fort Griffin* by Charles Robinson III, both of which contained accounts of the Larn murder.

There are, as already stated, a number of personal accounts of the event. Henry Herron's account is noteworthy: "But for some reason I was not put on guard that night. Probably it was a lucky thing for me that I was not for I did not believe in mob law and had often stated that I would not give up a prisoner regardless of the offense committed. That night Larn was shot to death at the jail." Larn was twenty-nine years old at the time of his killing, and it was the last one committed by the vigilantes in Shackelford County. It remains an event cloaked by mystery and unanswered questions although time and time again good historians and western writers have retold parts of the story, always in slightly different versions, always leaving out part of the puzzle. No one seems to have gotten the story all together yet. After 123 years, it is doubtful anyone will!

Poe, a buffalo hunter who operated out of Griffin with John Jacobs and Joe McCombs, later became a prominent banker and businessman of Roswell, New Mexico. From Fort Griffin, Poe went to Mobeetie and was hired by Pat Garrett as a deputy in hunting down the infamous Billy the Kid. One night Poe was on the porch of Pete Maxwell's house in Fort Sumner, New Mexico, when Garrett killed the Kid inside the house.

Selman rode west to become part of the Evans Gang that ran a cattle rustling operation in the Davis Mountains. Later, after having lived with his family in Mexico for some time, he saw the error of his ways and became a peace office in El Paso, only to be shot and killed after a drunken conversation with the Deputy U. S. Marshall responsible, George Scarborough. It was while Selman was in El Paso that he killed the infamous bad man of the time, John Wesley Hardin.

Jacobs moved to San Antonio where he made a sizable fortune raising and selling polo ponies. McCombs lived out his life in Albany where two of his granddaughters, Pollye Wheeler and Beth Snyder, and other descendants still live.

It is a testament to the concerns of these early citizens that at a time when the county was occupying an $800 picket courthouse, the court voted to build an $8,000 stone jail one block east of the square. Thomas and Woerner of Fort Worth were selected as contractors. A small house just south of the courthouse belonging to County Judge Ledbetter was rented for a temporary jail. This is where Larn met his fate and would place it on the lot of or across the street from

Harold Law's old Chevron station. Herron who often served as a deputy sheriff describes it:

> The first jail at Albany was a box house 12 by 14 feet and was located on the northwest corner of the second block south of the square. We had from ten to eighteen men in this jail most of the time, and they were in there for every kind of an offense, ranging from fighting to horse stealing and murder, but not many for murder. Before a man was placed in this jail or guard house, he was first taken to Charley Reinbold's blacksmith shop, and irons or shackles would be riveted to his legs. He was then placed in jail and allowed to run around the building during the daytime, but at night a chain was run between the prisoner's legs above the shackles, and one end of the chain was fastened securely to either end of the jail. The prisoners were guarded both day and night, and there were never less than two deputies on duty and we never lost a prisoner by escape from this guard house.

25

The sheriff needed an office and A. Carey offered to build one next to the courthouse and furnish all materials for a cost of ninety-five dollars. This did not eliminate the problem of the flimsy courthouse, and it continued to be a problem. Not only was it so cold in the winter that court could not be held, but neither was it secure. Vandals damaged the building and on one occasion a reward was offered of $150 for "those who willfully and maliciously broke the windows of the courthouse." Thieves broke in, pried open a desk drawer, and stole an unspecified sum of county money. Repair of the structure was a constant nuisance, the stove needed repair regularly, too, and wood had to be hauled. Quickly, another addition of six feet was added on the east end of the sheriff's office as space for the county officers, "to be paid for out of the first available fund that may be in the Treasury," and to be built by Charles Bailluch for $350.

When the county attorney, J. W. Wray, resigned, Stribling led a petition to appoint J. N. Browning. Browning came from Arkansas. He also lived at Fort Davis during the war and studied law under Stribling at Fort Griffin. Later, Browning served four terms in the Texas Legislature and became lieutenant governor of Texas under Governor Sayers.

Edgar Rye started the first newspaper in Albany called *The Tomahawk*. Rye attended county court regularly and was obviously interested in politics and county affairs as the following item from the February 28, 1879, issue of *The Tomahawk* will attest. "Ink flowed freely in the court room Thursday evening, but we do not think any thing tangible was produced." He became a careful observer of county affairs. While no significant growth occurred, it became apparent when the buffalo slaughter ended and when Albany citizens raised $50,000 to win the railroad, that Fort Griffin's future was doomed. Just as the soldiers left Fort Griffin for a last time in 1881, the Texas Central Railway arrived in Albany, although the Western Trail was still being used for cattle drives.

The first presiding judge, C. K. Stribling, ran for and won as county judge replacing Judge Ledbetter. When he retired after a two-year term, an adulatory, well-worded testimonial spread across the minutes concerning Stribling's character and "the efficient, prompt, and faithful manner in which he has discharged the duties . . . [with] genial disposition and moral excellence of character . . . [and] wise counsel and clear judgment." On taking office once again as county judge, he immediately initiated a petition of county citizens addressed to Governor O. M. Roberts and asking the county to declare that Shackelford County was no longer a "frontier county" and that the law prohibiting the unlawful carrying of firearms be enforced. The court agreed that the county was no longer subject to Indian raids and therefore was not a "frontier county." It is obvious that county officials wanted to eliminate firearms from being carried by the public.

Robson continued to promote Fort Griffin through his paper, but some of his comments concerning the conduct of Griffin citizens betray the actual condition of the town. In January 1881, "*The Echo* mildly suggests that the practice some people have of leaving scales, boxes, barrels and barbed fence wire on the side-walk, wagons in front of shops, throwing ashes, water (in freezing weather), old boots and tin cans into the street, be discontinued." Despite feuding with Edgar Rye, Robson moved his newspaper to Albany where it became *The Albany Echo*. Other businesses moved to be near the railroad, some along with their buildings such as the Rye-Caperton House on the east side of the square. Few other than the Tonkawas were left at Griffin and over time ranchers took the rock from buildings of the town until only the Masonic Hall and one frame store, the Fort Griffin General Merchandise, remained. In the 1970s the latter also moved to Albany to become a popular restaurant. Today the once rollicking and lively supply point on the cattle trail is but a ghost town, however, recently the Masonic Hall that burned in the 1980s has been restored by the new owners of the Griffin town site, Lynne Teinert and her husband, Clifford.

Nursing a grudge with Edgar Rye's newspaper, George Robson proclaimed that he had gone to ABILENE "the future great," and that the town "bids fair to rival its Kansas namesake as a cattle mart." To further that impression, Abilene extended a cordial invitation via *The Echo* to the people of Taylor and adjoining counties to attend a grand barbecue at that thriving village on Monday, July 4th: "Oodles of fun and rational enjoyment will be provided. Mr. George Soule, mail contractor between here and Abilene, will put on extra horses and hacks and carry passengers on this occasion for five dollars the round trip. Hurrah for the

26

1885

27

Fourth of July! Hurrah for Abilene and George Soule!" As it turned out, Abilene's railroad, the T&P coming from the east, did prove to be more successful than Albany's railroad, and Robson's remarks were much more prophetic in this case than similar remarks had been about Fort Griffin.

Albany lawyer Archibald A. Clarke had a hand in luring the railroad from Fort Griffin to Albany. Clarke, a native of Tennessee, rendered services for some of the more colorful names on the frontier: Lottie Deno, Dr. R. B. Lignoski, Frank Conrad, T. E. Jackson, John Jacobs, Henry Herron, John C. Lynch, A. W. Duffy, Bill Cruger, the Franco-Texas Land Co. and the Texas Central Railway. His obituary tells that a scouting party was out looking for a terminus of the Texas Central. The party spent several days at Fort Griffin and had about decided that Griffin would be the terminus when they accidentally discovered that it was built on "overflow territory" of the Clear Fork, so the group came to Albany, and Judge Clarke made the deal. Seven months after the soldiers left Fort Griffin for a last time, the red cars pulled by H. & T. C. Engine No. 49 of the Texas Central Railway arrived in Albany on December 16, 1881.

Still, the Western Cattle Trail was handling huge numbers of cattle and had replaced the Chisholm Trail as the one most used in Texas. Subsequent fencing had all but eliminated the trails to the east and as it crept westward, one could easily foretell the prominence of railroads and barbed wire.

As the terminus of the Texas Central for nineteen years, Albany and the county prospered. Each train brought new people and even a new town—Hulltown—fifteen miles southeast of Albany, later renamed Moran after the president of the Texas Central. *The Echo* crowed, "The daily trains are laden with 10 to 15 car loads of lumber to meet the unprecedented demand for building material. Buffalo bones for fertilizer and thousands of tons of limestone blocks for building stone were returned by these same trains" Robson bragged even further, "Building rock is found in the hills in close proximity to town. Several hundred thousand tons of this rock were shipped to Houston last summer, for building bridge piers and paving the streets of that city, this showing its superiority over rock much nearer Houston." New businesses sprang up such as John C. Lynch's rock two-story building attached on the west to the older 1878 section, built on Fannie's lot. Both sections of the building are now known as the Lynch Building. In the early 1970s, Clifton Caldwell purchased the building from J. Carter King, a grandson of L. H. Hill, and restored the handsome two-storied stone building. This started a domino effect in Main Street restoration. Soon after, Jim Cotter restored the Bailluch Building.

J. C. Lynch ran 3,000 longhorns on the open range then called Cow Valley on Hubbard Creek. Generous to a fault and well liked, he hated war and refused to fight in the Civil War, though he took Sam Houston's side against secession. Albany and Hulltown experienced a boom in growth and construction, but the train also brought an unwanted guest—smallpox.

An 1882 epidemic devastated the county treasury and several victims died. The county made a plea to the state for money. An isolated pest house flying a yellow flag was set up for quarantined victims, and a separate cemetery south of town was opened for their burials. The sheriff was ordered by the court to furnish provisions for those removed to the house including "mattresses, blankets, and cooking utensils as well as medical care." Despite setbacks, Albany citizens remained optimistic. The newspapers promoted the town continually. Rye continued to be associated with *The Tomahawk* through a succession of other names and partners. First as the *Western Sun* then as the *Albany Sun* (1880–82), he campaigned through the printed word to replace the pitiful picket courthouse. He drew cartoons and made wood cuts depicting it as embarrassing to Albany.

In one such drawing there are five men huddled around a wood-burning stove. The caption says: "This rough sketch (the result of using our pen-knife on the reverse side of a patent medicine advertisement) is not intended to reflect on honorable gentlemen who are members of our commissioners court, whom we entertain the greatest respect. It is the Court ROOM and NOT court, that we desire to place on exhibition, for we are satisfied strangers visiting our town would like also to visit the court room." Rye continued doing woodcut cartoons with *The Albany Star* (1883), and Robson, *The Echo* man, put aside differences with Rye and joined the verbal campaign. All of these newspapers ultimately became *The Albany News*. Rye was elected county attorney in November 1882 and just after he took office, sentiment to build a new courthouse had developed among county citizens.

As this was happening, the county treasurer's books were found deficient. In January 1883, the twelve sureties on the bond of W. C. Pace were notified that there were errors in the books. Many of the sureties were either current or past county officials. Evidence pointed to his having absconded with several thousand dollars, but a suit for embezzlement wasn't filed for another year.

On February 15, 1883, Commissioner R. A. Elliott (great-grandfather of present Judge Ross Montgomery) made the following motion: "That when this court adjourn . . . each commissioner ascertain from the tax payers . . . their sentiments concerning the building of a courthouse and when the court convins [sic] next to report to the court the names of those who are in favor and those who are in opposition to building."

On February 16, 1883, Edgar Rye drew the "Peep Into the Court House" cartoon and wrote a very strong editorial declaring "Court House! Court House!" in the *Albany Star*. Headlines were seldom used by papers of the day. A commentary of sorts in the same issue reminded taxpayers to sign the courthouse petition, "since the sentiment of the people must be taken. If you are for the erection of it put your name on the left, and if you are against it, let your autograph stand out in bold relief to the right. As the matter stands now, the largest number of the taxpayers represented and presented to the commissioner's court on the 12th of March, will settle the matter, and we hope all will take a lively interest in the enterprise, and give the court what they seek to wit: a full expression from its constituents. A Courthouse is a necessity and Shackelford County will never find a better time to build it than now."

Rye never let up in his writing and is credited with bringing down the picket courthouse. As a response to Elliott's motion, county officials circulated the petition on whether or not to build a new courthouse. It seemed important in everyone's mind. The ayes won and the court lost no time in moving on it. How sad that the petition has been lost! No record exists of the tally or the names of those who signed.

On March 13, 1883, Commissioner Barre made the motion that finalized plans for construction:

> Whereas the present Court House does not afford sufficient safety for the records of the county and room for the courts and officers of the county, and that interest bearing bonds be issued in accordance with

the law in the amount that may be set by the court and negotiated for cash to the best advantage to the county for the purpose of erecting a suitable Court House.

Seconded by Frank Conrad, it passed unanimously.

Though court sessions are not recorded in February, it is evident discussions had taken place previously because on March 14 the court selected plans presented by architect J. E. Flanders of Dallas. Stipulations were made that the structure would cost no more than $27,000, and if it did exceed that sum the architect's fee of $1250 would not have to be paid; the building would be 60 x 80 ft. and built of stone; and the architect would make ten trips to Albany during construction. Flanders would file a duplicate set of plans with the clerk and have sureties of $20,000.

30

James E. Flanders was educated in the Chicago public schools. His father was a carpenter. Five years after the great fire of Chicago, and enticed to wanderlust by tales of a booming Dallas, Flanders moved and set up his practice in 1876. By using the knowledge of drafting, carpentry, and engineering he had acquired as an apprentice with established masters in Chicago, he quickly made a name for himself as an architect of houses, churches, and courthouses. He may have been responsible for as many as fifteen courthouses, but only two remain, of which Shackelford County is the only one left from his nineteenth century work. The Navarro County Courthouse is an example of his twentieth century work. His masterpiece in Dallas was the Trinity Methodist Church that burned in the 1980s. The Methodist Church in Stamford is still another example of his skill.

The county moved swiftly during the next two months, setting a "tax of 25 cents on $100 for the Court House," approving Flanders' plans, and advertising for bids on the courthouse in *The Albany Star*, *The Daily Galveston News*, and *The Daily Dallas Herald*. Other county activity concerned an election at Fort Griffin to bar "sale of intoxicating liquors and medicated bitters producing intoxication." The majority voted *for* Prohibition. The court met frequently and handled more extemporaneous items such as a May 28 order that the Texas Central Railway "remove all dead cattle near their stock pens and not to leave any more at pens in or near Albany." Of primary concern was the deficiency of county funds. Finances weren't the best to be undertaking such an ambitious building project. But, despite recording only $330.39 cash in the county treasury, commissioners rented a building on the northeast corner of the square to use during construction. This is where the Ice House Restaurant now is located.

Of the nine bids received, the low one of $27,900 from C. Harris and Co. of Seymour, Baylor County, was selected; however, Flanders was not denied his architectural fee. Firm members were Calvin Harris, J. W. Foley, and Charles

Holman. Sureties in addition to the company principals were Lewis Casner, J. Casner, G. F. Atkinson, H. M. Childress, C. J. Christopher, W. B. Mills, J. B. Yarborough, P. A. Tackitt and D. J. Findly. Edgar Rye was unanimously appointed as Superintendent of Courthouse Construction at fifty dollars a month. His qualifications for the job are difficult to determine, but it is clear the county officials maintained confidence that he could do the job.

This notice appeared in *The Albany Echo*: "Be it remembered that on Thursday, June 21st, 1883, the first stone was dressed and the first shovel full of earth removed for the foundation of the new court house. Harris & Co. are not letting grass grow under their feet. Within twenty-four hours after their bond was approved they had men quarrying stone, teams hauling and cutters dressing. Hurrah for Harris & Co.! Hurrah for the new court house! When can we hurrah for a good school house?" These were ambitious folk!

The public square needed to be prepared for construction activities, and in the June 22nd court minutes, E. R. Manning and F. E. Conrad were ordered to "remove all posts placed on the Courthouse Square by them or through them. They must be moved away on or before six weeks from this date." On the same day *The Albany Star* reported, "The Old Court House is gone. Charley Hartfield moved it away last Wednesday to the rear of his restaurant and we are informed that he purposes to use it for lodging rooms for parties working on the Court House." Hartfield purchased the picket structure at public auction for $80, and the money was added to the prisoner's fund.

The Hartfield Building now stands where Charley's restaurant was just across the street west from the courthouse and is currently the Momentum Oil Company, formerly the Masonic Lodge Building and office of the Stasney Oil Company. It is a handsome two-storied stone building, recently purchased and restored by Lynn Neff, Mike Parsons, Don and Bob Tidwell, all Albany residents.

"The ring of the Mason's hammer can be heard cutting the water tables for the foundation," as Rye's newspaper agreed that the contractors had started off working diligently. Flanders made a visit and was well pleased with the work.

Joe Blanton, Albany architect and authority on church organ case design, wrote in his 1983 booklet, *The County Builds a Courthouse*, that the foundation depth is quite shallow. He quotes a handwritten note on the drawings now located at the Old Jail Art Center that "All foundations to have uniform depth of 2 feet below the surface of the ground at the North East corner of the building and brought to a level thereto under all walls with all defective spots or soil taken out to be natural concrete and refilled with a concrete of gravel and Ft. Scott cement." Blanton explains the "natural concrete" referred to is a "stratum of caliche underlying most of Albany." This has been verified during the recent restoration when a hole had to be dug on the northeast corner of the building to install utility and plumbing lines. A well dug on the northwest corner of the square in 1877 by William Norton went through 19 1/2 feet of hard stone and 22 1/2 feet of soap stone or fire clay.

The Echo announced in July, "It is reported to us that the wire fences of Reynolds & Matthews have suffered a little by being cut, but the work is supposed to have been done by parties who were passing through the country and could not find the gates or knew nothing of them." Life moved on. The Albany Coronet Band played. The Shields Opera House had performances. Community sings were held. Many homes and businesses were being built along with churches. A bank started up, two large cattle companies organized, enrollment at the school stood at 165, a cemetery opened, and arrivals at the Central Hotel were posted weekly in the newspapers.

Hulltown, situated on Deep Creek, was humming, too. Albany youth went there for picnics dressed in lavender pants and kid gloves. Mr Hull came to town and reported to The Echo that his town, "15 miles below here is small but loud and business [is] good."

Sorrow came, too. Word was received that W. R. "Bill" Cruger had been killed in a shoot-out in Princeton, Kentucky. The Star said, "Few men who have lived in this county commanded greater respect and esteem than did William R.

32

CIRCA 1909

Cruger. Quiet and unassuming—he was brave as a lion and dared to go wherever duty called him. . . . Perhaps his relatives and friends living at his old home in Albany, Georgia, will never know how kindly he is remembered among the pioneers of Albany, Texas." Also, one of the county's founding fathers died, Judge W. H. Ledbetter. A resolution on his behalf is recorded in the court minutes.

The court met frequently, but trouble quickly arose. Rye disagreed with the sand quality the contractor was using, and the court insisted the specifications be closely followed. Admittedly, George Robson in *The Albany Echo* bragged on Rye's work, but complained that, "In connection with some of our county officials we learn that the subject of laying the cornerstone of the court house with appropriate ceremonies had not been thought of. This may be everybody's business, if so, nothing will be done, but it occurs to us a cornerstone properly baptized with corn and wine would be the proper thing." No record exists that this was ever carried out.

Availability of money was an issue throughout construction. Judge J. R. Fleming, a banker and lawyer, acted as agent in selling bonds, "at no charge against the County," but troubles continued until during the second week of August work ceased on the structure altogether. The workers had not been paid. The contractors appeared before the court asking "permission to make the record room windows different from those specified." The court replied that strict compliance with the plans must be maintained. Cleaning off the square included selling the privy. The sheriff was ordered to receive cash and, "exercise his judgment in selling said privy to best advantage for the county." Again, Charles Hartfield bought it and moved it behind his place of business.

The county clerk was ordered to telegraph Fleming to ask if the bonds were ready, how to draw against them and where to place them. James R. "Dick" Fleming was born in 1848 in Kentucky. He became a drummer boy in the Civil War at the age of thirteen, and after coming to Texas in 1866, became quite well known in area politics as a district judge, an entrepreneur, and a monetary manager. Evidently Fleming didn't reply to the court's query because the next day the court paid expenses of Commissioner R. A. Elliott to travel to Cisco and ask the judge whether or not the Shackelford County Courthouse bonds had been negotiated. Within a couple of weeks the county had sold $10,000 worth of bonds with Nelson & Noel of St. Louis and placed the money in Fleming's bank in Cisco. At that time Albany had only a newly organized private bank of which Fleming also was president and major stockholder. The courthouse bonds were payable at the banking house of John J. Cisco & Co. of New York.

The county then paid $1900 to the contractor over the $4000 already paid. Two local businessmen, John C. Lynch and J. H. Biggs, had loaned the initial sum of $4000 to begin construction. The stone work foreman had ten

33

cutters, four masons, and six laborers and was hoping to have six more cutters in another week. Three carpenters were working. Obviously, the men were paid because they quickly completed the windows and framing of the doors of the first floor. For those who know anything about rock work, it is clear that the amount of work required for the amount of stone used would be a test of endurance and stamina even in our automated, mechanical, and technical world.

The Albany Star brags that the "Messrs. C. Harris and Co. have gone to work on the new Court House like men of business. They are men of toil and acquainted with work and you bet will build the Albany Court House." The Echo man, Robson, chimed in, too, "If any man in Albany earns his money it is Edgar Rye Esq."

Using records and sources heretofore unknown and in his possession, Joe Blanton wrote this about the stone for the building in his 1983 booklet:

> The stone came from what now is the L. F. Hooker Ranch, a short distance southwest of Albany. On the back of a statement dated February 15, 1884, from H. C. Jacobs to the county for 1087 perch of stone at 20 cents a perch is this pencilled notation: "Notify Mr. Jacobs and Mr. Conner to furnish Certificate of the land from the Surveyor establishing their lines—to settle dispute where rock came from." Pinned to the statement is Flanders' certificate that there are 1087.7 perch of stone between water table and first belt course. Also pinned to it is the County Surveyor's certificate that "the rock for the Court House have been got and are now, on the S 1/2 of Sec. No. 16 and 22 and N 1/2 of Sec. No. 27 Block 11 T&P Railroad Co. Surveys." The quarrying and hauling of the rock was contracted at $1.10 a perch.... Stonecutters received $5 a day, stonemasons and stonecutters $4.50 a day, carpenters from $2.25 to $3.25 a day, and laborers from $1.50 to $2.25 a day.

The term "perch" is chiefly a British measurement for stone—one perch is equivalent to 24 1/2 cubic feet. The stone was hauled by mules and wagons with A. F. Corbin in charge. He had fourteen men and six teams hauling the stone from the quarry.

On September 7 the contractors dropped a bombshell when they notified the court that they were financially unable to complete construction but stated that they would not abandon the contract. After great deliberation with legal counseling from A. A. Clarke, the county decided to hire Edgar Rye at $100 a month to finish the building, with the county judge and four commissioners serving as the building committee. The county was adamant, "Nothing in the order should be construed," they recorded in the court minutes, "to release C.

Harris & Co. and their sureties from any obligations and penalties from the contract and bond." Bills were paid and Lynch received a payment on the money owed him.

One week later *The Star* reported this, "The contractors for the court house signed the order . . . to terms by which the county took charge of the work. . . . Under the present arrangement the workmen get their pay each week, thereby enabling them to meet their weekly living expenses, making things more pleasant for all parties. The . . . court displayed their usual good judgment in the selection of Mr. Rye as the general superintendent of the work."

Judge Fisher took a ten-day leave of absence, but in spite of it, additional men were hired and work continued. *The Albany Star* commented that "Work on the Court House seems to progress rather slowly from some cause." Perhaps blame should go to a celebration staged in early October when *The Echo* reported, "Monday afternoon and night a goodly number of the workmen on the Courthouse were on a high lonesome; next morning some of them were discharged and others quit the job but enough remain to carry on the work."

By the end of November, the walls for the first story of the courthouse were up and the second floor joists had been laid. A new elevator for hoisting stone to position worked daily.

Albany was experiencing prosperity. F. E. Conrad & Co., on the west side of the square, advertised they had the following items available: 200 bolts bleached domestic; 200 suits; 1 car full patent flour; 1 half car of patent flour; 1 car 4 X flour; 1 car Kansas meal; 1 car sugar and molasses; 1 car Rio coffee; 1 mixed car of apples, onions, cabbages, and sour kraut; 1 car Irish Potatoes; Buffalo Robes— all kinds & prices; 300 pairs blankets; and 1 mixed car of hams and bacon.

Beer was priced at 5 or 15 cents a glass at the local saloons. A variety of liquors, wines, and brandies were offered as well as unusual food items such as oysters, hauled to West Texas in barrels from the coast.

Flanders and Rye began having noticeable differences as evidenced by a November 29 court entry. Flanders demanded that Edgar Rye "remove at once the iron ventilators under the piers dividing the four pairs of double windows on each of the North and South elevations and fill with solid masonry." Shortly afterward, the court discovered that wording on plans and specifications had been altered without consent and knowledge of the court, but it is unrecorded as to who was responsible. The architect left the estimate of labor and material furnished to date at $13,471.88. He was paid $200 for plans, and Corbin was paid $200 for mules and wagons to haul stone.

The court requested that "Ed Rye ascertain what is the amount of the debt incurred by C. Harris & Co. on account of the Court House giving as nearly as possible an itemized statement thereof."

A low bid for the iron, cornice, and metal roof of $3100 came in by Huey & Philp of Dallas, but construction went at a slower pace in winter. County Judge Fisher asked for and received a twenty day leave of absence. It is apparent that this was regular procedure for him.

To relieve the monotony of bad weather *The Echo* regularly commented on everyday life, "While prowling about F. E. Conrad and Co.'s store the other day, we counted sixty-two barrels of sugar. Pretty good stock for one house in a small town to carry." "A large lot of hoop skirts just arrived at Manning's." And this item, "A number of Tonks took a Christmas frolic in Albany." Maybe they, too, wanted to see the new big rock building that was changing the appearance of the town they had watched come into existence. After years of relocating and massacre by other tribes as well as whites, the Tonkawa tribe still lived at Fort Griffin where they had served as scouts for the army. The tribe had always been helpful and friendly to white settlers.

In February 1884, *The Echo* commented on this subject for a second time, "The inhabitants of the western part of town are suffering the tortures of a bagpipe." Such names as McDonnell (sometimes misspelled as McDonald), O'Donnell, Campbell and Sullivan in payment records verify the presence of Scottish stonemasons and cutters at work on the courthouse. With the vantage of years, we can only say that the little bit of bagpipe music to be heard in the streets of Albany was little nuisance to suffer in return for receiving the splendid architectural gift left by these superb craftsmen.

A portion of Joe Blanton's description for the architectural section of the National Register Nomination in 1974, depicts the courthouse as follows:

> The Shackelford County Courthouse . . . is in the Victorian style (now considered a Second Empire structure) but of a design superior to most of its contemporaries in that its mass and proportions are better. The architect . . . achieved this by a more studied relationship of voids to solids, eschewing the highly elongated windows common to the style and avoiding the abundance of extraneous ornamentation usually appended to structures of the period. Without loss of any of the flavor of the Victorian, a feeling of massive solidity has been gained from the sheer size of the blocks of stone; those of the trim are skillfully dressed to give an interesting contrast to the rough-faced ashlar of the walls.
>
> The major facades on the north and south are of five-part composition with the minor ones on the east and west in three parts. The corner compartments project in both directions and the three exterior corners of each have finely dressed quoins throughout the entire three

stories. . . . Several vermiculated stones give variety to the doorways. The window heads of the second and third stories [sic] are segmental arches, each with a keystone of normal proportions and a single wide voussoir on each side. . . . Other examples of the excellent stone cutting which should not be overlooked are the huge splash blocks.

The edifice is in every way a hand-carved masterpiece, as much a work of art as any painting or sculpture. The reports of books and magazines tell us our courthouse is admired by all those who see or know about the structure. No doubt we have to thank in major part the Scotsmen who did the stonework. Local folklore tells us the stone craftsmen left Albany for Austin where the new Capitol was just breaking ground, and in comparing the stone work, we have every reason to believe it. It is known, however, that Patrick McDonnell stayed in Albany for a while and built the old City Grocery Building, the two-story Jacobs-Hill Building, and finished construction of the Hartfield Building after Hartfield committed suicide.

The Albany Echo recorded on January 1, 1884, that "The latest fine production of Metz, the photographer, is a picture of the court house taken on the 5th inst., which for artistic beauty, shows great skill in the artist." One month later it reported, "Corner walls to be built 16 ft. higher than at present. Mr. St. Clair [Sinclair] says he can have the stone work on the court house finished in a month, if we have pleasant weather." Reports given by Flanders estimated cost of the courthouse about $17,210, but the actual expense was about $20,000. The court retained the tax rate at twenty-five cents on $100 for the courthouse.

One year after finding discrepancies in their books, the county sued W. C. Pace, former county treasurer, for embezzlement. A petition was brought to court by the Monroe Cattle Co. and 360 other citizens of Shackelford County asking that the sureties of W. C. Pace be relieved of their responsibilities. The petition was rejected. This must have been a local controversy of an extreme nature for it wasn't settled until July when eight sureties agreed to pay 45 cents on the dollar. Judges C. K. Stribling and W. H. Ledbetter were among them along with John Jacobs and T. H. Barre.

Aside from this rather spectacular case, the bulk of legal issues before the county court dealt with noticeably tamer issues than those in contention ten years previously. For example, one case in dispute concerned the ownership of an eight-year-old brown horse. Another case involved the attempt to collect an unpaid account for "a Billiard Table, a pegion [sic] Hole Table, 8 kinds of cigars (all listed), 11 bottles of liquor including Absinthe, Annisette [sic], and Bordeaux, and wine and whisky by the gallon including Sour Mash Whisky, Sherry, Gin, and Apple Brandy."

CIRCA 1911

Sheriff's Office

Everyday life continued in Albany regardless of the big construction project going on, though it must have been the main subject of conversation at the Texas Central Saloon, at the Central Hotel right across the street, or in the Office Saloon or Burnett's Picture Gallery. The square was nicely filled in with thriving business houses. Businessman N. H. Burns was handling the need for increased water and submitted petitions for permission to lay and maintain underground water lines in the streets.

At the courthouse work continued and progressed. J. A. McAmis was awarded the painting contract at $1145 and John F. Broxton got the plastering contract for $888. It wasn't until March 1884 that the county received a perspective of how the building would look when completed. *The Albany News* quotes Mr. Sinclair, the stone superintendent, "The building will stand for 500 years if not destroyed by fire or providential interference." *The News* continued, "We have in the last month heard the remark made by strangers who have traveled all over the state, some of them practical mechanics and contractors, that Shackelford County will have when it is completed the finest and most substantive court house in the State of Texas." The stone work ended in March and already civic pride in the new building was a common theme in the newspapers.

The newspapers seemed to direct much of the work from the printed word. *The News* suggested "Why should not the small rock now scattered over the courthouse yard be hauled on the street? There is enough of chipping and gravel to make a good Macadamized road all around the square and from one end of Main Street to the other." There is no information as to whether this was done.

April came in with unseasonably cool weather and *The News* reported, "It was too cold yesterday for the workmen engaged in putting up the frame of the tower of the court house to work. The present height is about seventy feet. When completed it will be 115 ft. high."

The list of the workers who were paid that month are: John O'Donnell, H. Lieby, C. A. Hartfield, Wm. Campbell, Alf Sullivan, R. E. Millikin, C. C. Corbin, A. R. Manning, T. V. Baker, P. T. Glover, M. I. Jones, Joe Ezell, Stone (W. P.) & Cullum, H. C. Jacobs, J. G. Royle, J. A. McAmis, Edgar Rye, J. C. Lynch, T. P. Tackett, M. R. Bruckner, F. E. Conrad, W. E. Wigley, I. M. Chism, A. F. Corbin, S. Freeman, N. H. Burns, J. W. Manning, J. P. Lasley, J. T. Camp, W. S. Dalrymple, Clark & Clark, and Stone & Moore.

In addition, J. H. Biggs received $889.12 and J. C. Lynch $2,353.14 cash. A fair assumption can be drawn that this is final repayment for the money advanced to start construction.

Evidently, the Western Cattle Trail was still very much in use, for *The News* reported that "a 50,000 herd of cattle is blockaded near Albany waiting for the Clear Fork to go down."

The News reported a diversion of sorts when a giant tooth was found in the shoal of the Clear Fork at Fort Griffin weighing 2 lbs. 11 oz. and measuring 7 inches long, 2 1/2 inches broad, and 3 inches thick. John McLean of Throckmorton had it at press time.

Once again fireworks occurred between Rye and Flanders. The court recorded, "It appearing to the court that a misunderstanding exists between the architect and local supt. as to the work on the Court House, the clerk is instructed to notify the local supt. to discontinue all work on the Court House in such matters and particulars as are the subject of the misunderstanding."

In a now very delicate and faded letter that is part of the Robert Nail Archives in the Old Jail Art Center placed there in 1987 by Joe Blanton, Flanders writes to the court:

> To The Honorable Commissioners Court of Shackleford [sic] Co. Texas—Gentlemen, Upon an inspection of the work being done in the erection of your courthouse, made the 4th. Inst. I wish to state that I find the anchoring rods specified for the roof trusses, have been omitted, when they should have been built into the walls. I also find that the work is not progressing to the interest of Shackleford [sic] County, and the present superintendent is inclined to work in changes, not only as a reflection upon me as an architect, but also in my opinion, to the detriment of the building, and the prolonging of the work. For this reason I protest against the further employment of the present superintendent, as I cannot be responsible for work done by inexperienced men, I do not want any more jobs as Nolan County.

41

He finished his letter by recommending someone in Dallas (unnamed) for the job whom he trusts and although the letter is typed, a hand written note by his signature indicates he was also displeased with the painting job being carried on in the courthouse. Immediately *The Albany News* quotes Flanders, "It seems that a very gross blunder has been made and some body wants to shirk the responsibility."

At the recommendation of Flanders, Rye was relieved of his duties and requested to deliver all plans, specs, books, and papers pertaining to the courthouse and its transactions to the court. Although he had been fired, a positive recommendation of his work was placed in court minutes. Flanders wrote to immediately renege on his offer recommending a replacement and suggested the court hire Mr. Duffy, if possible, but evidently he was not available, and J. T. Camp took over at the same salary. Camp is basically an unknown. By this time, however, the building was nearly finished. Court orders that "plastering of lower rooms of Court House and District Court Room be finished with white coat and that the concrete floors be put in said plastering." For this work Broxton was paid $160.

The court requested that a total amount of the rock be determined by Flanders, and he gave these figures: perch of stone above the water table and including chimney tops and entrance steps, after deducting for openings was 42.915 cubic feet which equaled 2,600 perch. He ended the communication with a plea for money. "Please have court allow me $200 at next meeting. I have made 8 out of 10 visits and there is $550 due when the other two are made. I expect to make one or two extra visits without charge. Please do not forget me, as I have a note to meet, and am relying on you. I want to secure board for my wife and children (2) for two or three weeks in July. If you know of any private family where I can secure it, let me know."

We don't know if he brought his family to Albany to show off his latest handiwork or not. His stationery stated that he had courthouses in Dallas, Nolan, Eastland, Rockwell, Stephens, and Shackelford. None of these buildings except ours is still standing. Local belief has attributed Rye's insistence on using good sand as the reason the structure is standing. Engineers who have been to have a "look see" always comment on the foundation.

In a July letter to the court the architect summarized the work. The steps and tin and cornice work were excellent and fully up to specifications. The roof was another matter, however, and his comments concerning it were prophetic and not so easily handled as he thought. "There may be a few leaks in the roof, but the first rain will show them, and they can be easily stopped." He objected to the color of the district courtroom ceiling and suggested putting two more coats on it. The comment on the roof problem proved true when heavy rain caused slight damage to the district courtroom ceiling by water coming in through the tower and was reported in *The News*.

As the finishing touches were being put on the building, one of the workmen, Daniel Sheegro, fell from the scaffold about fifteen feet to the ground. Fortunately, he only severely strained his ankle. Another incident, as Joan Farmer recalls for us, had a more humorous tone. *The News* reported, "Last Sunday, Porter Barre and some other boys were inspecting the courthouse vaults, and just to see whether everything worked all right, Porter stepped inside and tole [sic] some of the other boys to shut the vault door, which they did and turned the combination." After remaining in the vault for about an hour, Porter, who was badly scared, was freed by someone who knew the combination.

The court asked Flanders for names of lightning rod agents. A petition of 162 citizens was given to the court asking for a town clock to be placed on the courthouse, and the tower was modified for a belfry. The court accepted the bid of Howard Watch and Clock Co. at $1000. The clerk contacted Flanders to send plans for "stair, newel posts, stair railings for District Court Room and Judge Stands at once." Camp was to clean up the courthouse square, to sell off surplus lumber, and to place under lock and key in the courthouse all tools and ropes belonging to the county. The court refused the request of Flanders to return plans and drawings stating that they are "rightfully theirs."

The June 13 issue of *The News* described the ceiling of the district courtroom and it must have been a beauty. It was "in irregular panels [of wood] with a drop of fourteen inches, and will require a car load of molding of different kinds to finish it."

Why was Rye fired so close to the end of the work? Clues to the answer are revealed in Flanders' letters and court records. The first clue is in his letter of November 10, 1884, to the court, his final report. It is a lengthy commentary on the courthouse work:

> I wish to say that those portions of the work coming under the following heads are fully up to the intent and meaning of the plans, specifications and contracts. The stone work; painting; and tin and galvanized iron work. In regard to the plastering and some portions of the carpenter work, notably the stairs, I am not so well satisfied .... As a whole, I think Shackelford County has the best courthouse in the State, for the cost, and one of which she may well feel proud. I have heard today that the acoustics of the main courtroom are not good. I cannot account for this, except by the increased height given the room, and which was not called for by the plans, and contrary to my idea of proper height for said room in connection with its other dimensions.

He suggested building a gallery as a way of making the ceiling seem lower and improving the acoustics.

Well, the gallery was never built, and Rye's ceiling stayed the height he had made it until it was lowered after collapsing in the 1950s. One can hardly blame Rye for the stairway. Time and again the court minutes reflect the county's frustration in getting drawings and specifications from the architect for the doors, windows, stair newel posts and stair railings for the district court room and judges' stands.

As late as March of 1884 the county had not seen a drawing of how the building would look when finished. Rye, with his "can-do" attitude and his responsibility for pushing the job along, probably was not wont to wait until the thin-skinned Flanders delivered necessary details. When the whole story is looked

43

CIRCA 1919

44

at, one would have to agree that Rye and Flanders were nothing alike in their approach to the building except in wanting a beautifully finished product.

Lightning rods were purchased from L. E. Morse (Moss), and he was "paid $200 for protecting the occupants of the new court house from annihilation by the electric fluid." Final payment on rock hauling was made. While waiting for the clock to be delivered, interior work was finished, including a repainting of the district courtroom ceiling in a lighter shade of blue. Pat McDonnell completed the stone steps, praised by the architect as the best stone work on the building.

The 800 pound bell was hoisted to its belfry in August, the clock ensconced, and blinds and sash installed in the courtroom. When the furniture arrived damaged from A. H. Andrews & Co. of Chicago, it was repaired and paid for by the company with A. W. Duffy in charge. Duffy was a superior builder who is responsible for the Ed Compton home, the Eddie Eddington home, and the original stone schoolhouse that stood where the football stadium is now. Robert Nail, creator of the *Fort Griffin Fandangle*, saw to it when the school was torn down that its stone was incorporated into the stadium, and because of this it is named for him.

Just as the work wound down the Albany newspapers made comments concerning some oversights. *The Albany News* of August 15, 1884, recorded, "The stairways over the east and west doors, and against the windows above, are sores to the eye—architecturally viewed even from the outside." And another issue gave cause for the comment, "The convenience of a water closet at the building or on the grounds has been neglected, whether intentional or not ye loke sayeth naught on the subject." But the sash was all in and the blinds had been put in position. So, coal was purchased and bills were paid. Inconveniences would have to be handled later. J. T. Camp, Rye's replacement, was jailed and fined in October for an unknown offense related to his job. D. G. Simpson finished the courthouse.

One wonders what the friendly Tonkawa Indians thought of the structure now that it was finished. Less than a hundred Indians—*The Albany News* reported ninety-three including a few Lipans—left Fort Griffin for the last time that month under the charge of Lieutenant Chandler, boarded the train in Albany on their way to Cisco, and then were taken to their reservation in the Indian Territory.

The county occupied the new building seventeen months after construction began. It must have been luxurious compared to the old picket structure. At last the county had a district courtroom worthy of Rye's aspirations. County Judge Fisher resigned just as R. M. Norman presented a bond and was sworn into office along with the other new county officials. Edgar Rye was re-elected county attorney. There was a turnover in commissioners. Criswell and Waters, replaced Barre and Elliott. Frank Conrad and C. H. Philbrick were held over, D. G. Simpson became sheriff and Sam Spears became county clerk.

Flanders made his final appearance before the court. *The Albany News* gave this report on November 21, "Architect J. E. Flanders was up last week. He tells us that the Stephens County Courthouse, the plans of which he prepared, is about finished, and while it is a good and substantive building it does not come up to Shackelford's house in architectural beauty. He says that our court house is generally considered the handsomest in middle Texas." We can only speculate as to what Edgar Rye was thinking.

The sheriff was ordered to gather up the old furniture, lumber, tools, etc. and sell them in a public auction, and he was paid $50 a year for winding the clock. Should he let it stop, he was to pay the start-up expenses. The essential stoves were placed within the assessor's office and other areas of the building. Chandeliers and carpet were purchased and placed in the district courtroom. A. W. Duffy and Son were paid $50.25 for the repair and installation of the furniture made by A. H. Andrews and J. W. Butler. Almost immediately, the county rented the northwest room of the second floor to Webb and Webb for office space at $12.50 a month payable in advance.

Flanders left on a high note, but he came back the following April to appear as a witness against the county in the lawsuit between the original contractor, C. Harris & Co. and Shackelford County. And, as far as the county's case went, he most assuredly wasn't a friendly witness. Harris filed a suit against the county for $8000, and the county cross-filed for a figure nearing $25,000. The ambitious and talented Rye was employed by the commissioners' court to assist L. W. Campbell with the case. During the litigation, it was revealed that the county

45

had sold $55,000 in bonds and estimated the actual cost of the building at $49,433.75, though when adding furniture and other finishing costs it probably took the entire amount to put the county in the building.

Rye had written in his application for building superintendent that he had "about five years practicable experience." Everyone knew he had ability. Again, Blanton used unknown references concerning the court proceedings. In testimony during the trial, the old animosity between Rye and Flanders surfaced once again. When Flanders was asked if an architect is different from a carpenter or a stonemason, Flanders took an acerbic stab at Rye. "Yes, there is a difference between an architect and a carpenter, or a stonemason, or a sign painter, or a wood engraver, or a lawyer, or a combination of all of these," he answered. He testified that the building had been constructed in an extravagant, impractical manner due to the "poor handling of work and men."

46

Not until 1887 did the county know the result of the litigation when Henry Palm, the jury foreman, announced in favor of the county. The lawsuit awarded $900 with 8% interest plus costs to total $1108.50 for Shackelford County. Joe Blanton called it a pyrrhic victory, but in West Texas we might say it was more or less a "stand off." The ironic part of the story is that both Flanders and Rye died and were buried in Hollywood, California.

The first large crowd to gather in the courthouse came to see and hear Clara Barton, founder of the American Red Cross. She came to Albany in 1887, to observe first-hand the drought conditions in northwest Texas. There is an interesting story behind her two-week stay in Shackelford County. After the railroad arrived, publicity was circulated which portrayed the advantages of owning West Texas land in tempting terms. Soon small farmers from the eastern states came to settle the land and till the soil for a living. Most of them came without cash because they had spent all they had to get here and lacked any means of returning once they saw the dismal situation and dry climate. Generally speaking, aside from an occasional good year, the county lands are not well suited for farming on a grand style. In a large *Albany News* article, Mrs. A. A. Clarke's daughter-in-law, Mary Clarke, wrote about Mrs. Clarke's remembrances of the drought and Miss Barton's visit: "Many of the larger land owners were not in sympathy with these smaller, less fortunate, folk. They felt that they were invaders. The former had pioneered the land, wrested it from the Indians and buffalo. They knew that it took a large range to fatten cattle and that water was a necessity."

The rain stopped in 1885 and there was no rain at all in 1886. The small farmers, called nesters, suffered more than the ranchers because their seed dried up and died without moisture for germination, and they also lost most of their small number of animals. There might have been a temptation on the part of the ranchers to let them suffer until they turned tail and returned to where they came from. The A. A. Clarkes came to Albany in 1877. Mr. Clarke was an early lawyer in the new county seat. Again, Mrs. Clarke described the drought, "The earth was cracked and as hard as the native limestone and overhead the sun beat down relentlessly day after day with no relief. The cattle died by the hundreds and their bones lay bleached upon the shriveled prairie grass. Those who could afford it had drinking water hauled in by rail, and drove their stock to water."

The Reverend John Brown, another Scottish native, had made his way from Boston, Massachusetts to the west, met the widow Mary Matthews Larn and married her. He was pastor of the Presbyterian Church in Albany. Reverend Brown became distressed over the wretched condition of many in his congregation. He decided to take action and boarded the train for Washington where he was able, in some way, to describe the hopeless situation to President Grover Cleveland. The President was so touched by the story that he called in Clara Barton to hear Brown retell the story of "the poor families who had come to Texas from other states thinking that this was the land of milk and honey ... as they'd been told by the land speculators."

47

Mrs. Clarke says that Miss Barton, who was an "elderly maiden lady," decided to come to Texas with the kind-hearted minister and her field agent, Dr. Hubbell, to see the conditions. She stayed with the George T. Reynolds family for two weeks, riding out in the countryside daily in a buckboard to visit the small landowners. She spoke to a very large crowd in the new Shackelford County Courthouse about the mission of the American National Red Cross and of the families she had visited here and of those in a calamitous recent flood in Mississippi.

Sallie Reynolds (Mrs. J. A.) Matthews wrote her Texas classic, *Interwoven*, after she was seventy years old. Her youngest child, Watt, died in 1997 at the age of ninety-eight. Lucille (Brittingham), a daughter, lived to a hundred and four years of age. Published in 1936 and written as an eye-witness account of the frontier, Sallie observed that Miss Barton was kind and sympathetic but firm in her belief that Texas could take care of its own and didn't need the Red Cross to intervene on their behalf. Sallie wrote that Barton felt, "Texas was too big and too resourceful to be calling for help outside the State. She also said that much of the money contributed to the Red Cross was the hard earned pennies of very poor people in the East, and intimated that we did not know what hard work was as the New Englander knew it, and that we were not thrifty and provident as they were. This she had learned, no doubt, from her visits in their homes. I think most of us agreed with her there."

Sallie described Barton as a "noble and distinguished guest ... an intelligent woman, a wise woman, a strong forceful speaker, pleasant and unassuming in manner." It was obvious that Mrs. Matthews was very impressed with Miss Barton as was Mrs. Clarke. There may have been some embarrassment concerning the nature of her visit, but everyone seemed to have benefited from the contact with her. The Shackelford County Commissioners Court responded by purchasing $500 worth of flour, corn meal, and bacon for hungry people plus $444.25 of corn for suffering animals.

On her way home, Barton stopped by to visit with Colonel Alfred Belo, founder and owner of *The Dallas Morning News*. She issued a lengthy statement letting the newspaper know, in so many words, that it was their responsibility to make people aware about such crises on their own doorstep. She announced that the Texas Legislature had appropriated $100,000 for food, and Congress had arranged to send $100,000 [or $10,000, depending on the source] worth of seeds to relieve the suffering. Barton ended her statement by saying, "I desire as I pass over the boundary line of Texas on my way to the East to feel that the people of this great and beautiful state have taken in hand this last want with a glad determination which shall in a few weeks put it forever out of sight."

Reverend John Brown and Mary left Albany and moved to New England the next year in spite of the Albany congregation pleading with them to stay. The newspaper printed sympathetic expressions of regret, "He will leave friends by the score who will not soon forget his noble, self-sacrifice last summer in his efforts to aid the drought sufferers. Many a hungry woman and child can thank John Brown for the food received while the terrible drought prevailed. He did what he conceived to be his duty fearlessly and regardless of anathemas heaped upon his head, and the people will not soon forget him."

In spite of the dry weather and the rough time for farmers, the Hulltown School could boast of forty-seven pupils, albeit they were of every age. Hulltown was given promise when M. D. Bray purchased the original town site from I. B. Scott. Still later, Bray with his brother-in-law, J. M. Rooks, operated a General Merchandise Store in Moran.

As for the new courthouse, from the beginning the roof presented a problem with repeated mention of repairs made in 1888, 1890, and 1893 and continuing into the next century. Court records reveal the county responded in a very responsible way concerning care of the building, but the large public square presented another problem because of the number of horses, cattle, and other unpinned animals in town. A. W. Duffy, Patrick McDonnell, and Edgar Rye were sent to inspect the roof in 1890. They obviously recommended action, but only one bid was received for $275 to paint it with asphalt and then apply white wash. Rye was appointed as inspector and superintendent of the work at no expense to the county. Evidently the work was a failure because three years later the county tried a new product on the market. Work was guaranteed on applying

Reeves Elastic Fire and Water Proof Roof Paint to the roof, dome, and belfry of the courthouse. Even under Edgar Rye's supervision the worrisome problem could not be solved, it seems.

The roaming animals were another irritating matter. To solve their intrusion, in 1903 *The News* reported "a beautiful iron fence will encircle our magnificent court house." This was accomplished by J. C. Taylor & Co. of Albany at a cost of over a thousand dollars. Previously, the wooden fence would not hold a white wash or keep the animals out. The new fence took care of animal problems for two years when it became necessary to put on new latches. *The News* once again commented, "Grass-eating animals have to hunt new pastures now." But, the roof remained a problem and in 1907 the court voted to repair the roof rather than replace it and that attempt lasted seven years.

From all appearances the Victorian times in Shackelford County were peaceful, happy years. Yet, things were changing. Hulltown was renamed Hicks in 1890 and renamed Moran two years later. By 1898, Moran had a hotel, four churches, a number of stores, a doctor, and two cotton gins. The sheriff still had the job of winding, oiling, and maintaining the courthouse clock, but his fee for doing this had been cut to twenty-five dollars a year. The sheriff also saw to cleaning and making necessary repairs when ordered to do so by the court. He seemed to have been given a great deal of leeway in doing his job, sometimes too much freedom perhaps. In August 1892, a curious entry appears in court minutes, "Ordered . . . the sheriff be and is hereby instructed not to rent any of the rooms of the court house for bed rooms, nor to allow any sleeping in any

49

CIRCA 1911

County Abstract Office

part of the Court House." There is no other clue as to what precipitated that concern. Additionally, the sheriff was asked to kill any and all pigeons found on the roof because they were polluting the cistern water supply.

Maintaining a pure water supply concerned everyone. Following the pigeon problem, the court hired N. H. Burns, local hardware dealer and founder of the Albany Water Works to furnish water for the tank on the square, supplying the hydrant on the courthouse yard with water for the trees and for the building, too. Water, as today, was a precious commodity, especially without the luxury of air-conditioning.

One way people had of circumventing the heat was to camp out-of-doors. In June of 1899, the Matthews and Reynolds families organized a camping party that seventy-six people attended. The tents were pitched near the springs at the mouth of Hurd Branch, half way between the Old Stone Ranch and the X Ranch headquarters at Round Mountain. Visits were made to the old ranch houses, and stories were told of Indian fights by actual participants. Three cooks worked to feed the crowd on fish and beef "barbecued to perfection by Chief Avery and his aides de camp."

Just before Christmas the circus came to town, and the Lemen Bros. Circus and Menagerie was held on the courthouse yard. The building and grounds were used for an assortment of purposes. The Albany Farmers Alliance used the southwest corner room on the third floor for their meetings. The Albany glee and mandolin clubs entertained the town folk. Baseball was popular.

Use of the courthouse was highlighted by inconsistencies. The yard was plowed and cultivated for a while, but one can only wonder what they grew. The court gave permission for the sheriff to have Parson Robinson use the courtroom to lecture in and "display the intelligence of a blind-folded girl and charging an admittance fee for same." At the same time the sheriff was told that he must "manage and control the courthouse as he has heretofore done." The road and bridge fund borrowed money from the Courthouse Fund to be repaid from taxes, and two courthouse bonds were paid off. A bounty on wolf scalps was kept at one dollar per scalp. During the later part of the Victorian period the court issued a ruling that ice cream suppers were damaging to the county's property and prohibited them from occurring on the courthouse yard. Throughout these years the court collected twenty cents per one hundred dollars valuation of property for the Courthouse Fund.

A new century arrived and the terminus of the Texas Central moved to Stamford. No longer did trains have to turn around in Albany. No longer was Albany the end of the line. This hurt some, but other economic advantages were in the wings. L. H. Hill and Sam Webb (Webb & Hill), real estate moguls, advertised that they had settled more people in the county in the last twenty-five years than all other agencies combined. Under their partnership in 1900, they bought the Goethe & Fuchs Ranch on the Clear Fork and laid off the town of Lueders, opening up the rock quarries and helping get the railroad extended from Albany to Stamford. Hill was born in Alabama and came to Texas in 1870. He started out in business by following the cattle trails to Dodge City, Kansas. Two of his grandsons, J. Carter King and Bill Hill, live in Albany. In 1882 the railroad brought W. G. Webb and his family, including Sam, to the S. O. Bull Ranch east of town. Today it is part of the Elliott place. Mr. Webb, born in Georgia, came to Texas in 1844 and was a veteran of the Mexican War. In 1860, Sam Houston appointed Mr. Webb as Brigadier General of the Texas Militia. Webb and his son Sam formed Webb & Webb in Albany, advertising they were in the "Law, Land, Livestock, and Loan" business. Sam and the late Graham Webb are grandsons of Sam Webb, and there are no descendants living in Albany today.

With the transition to 1900, the good old West Texas comment became reality that says "when it rains it rains like a damn fool." The news reported that there was "flooding and the Texas Central from North Hubbard Switch, a distance of ten or twelve miles, is terribly wrecked." Four or five bridges washed away and three miles of track. "It will be several days before the train can run again between Albany and Stamford as engine No. 108 was ditched and totally wrecked five miles west of Albany. Fireman Albert J. Johnson was instantly killed and the engineer had a narrow escape."

Jim Hair started up a newspaper in Moran called the *Moran Messenger*. Moran historian, Audrey Brooks, writes that strangers began to visit looking for oil and gas leases, and they knew the farmers and ranchers knew nothing about what to them was a new business. The money given for drilling rights, though of a small amount, was needed and appreciated. After fourteen months of very slow drilling, a new economic age came with the discovery in 1910 of the first commercial natural gas well in this vast area of West Texas, the Cottle No. 1, near Moran, opening commercial gas development.

Two years later it was piped in the courthouse by William Little at a cost of $500 "to do all piping, plumbing, furnishing stoves, light fixtures for heating and lighting, fitting connections, etc." Coal was out and gas was in. Gaslights also were placed on the four corners of the square.

The next year, buoyed with economic good times, the court built an outdoor "closet for the ladies." The following is the elaborate description of this structure in court minutes:

The Court is of the opinion that such building is necessary and it is therefore ordered by the Court that the said building be made 5 X 8 to be boxed and weather boarded with two compartments, with boxes to contain the refuse, and covered it with shingles, and screens running from the front corners coming nearly together in front, just leaving an opening or pass way and a screen shall be built back of and full length of said closet so as to protect the view from the street, said back screen to be four ft. high and the front screen to be six ft. high—said building to be painted together with the lattice screens.

Bert Brooks, grandfather of County Commissioner Jimmy Brooks of Moran, was hired to build the closet. Photographs show this outhouse located close to the building and just outside the east doorway.

Leasing for oil and gas provided extra cash and excitement. *The News* made known that Henry Green, Sam Webb, G. E. Waters, and W. M. Broyles had visited the Nail oil well and that it was down to 1,800 feet. They had commented there might be oil in the well. The Cottle No. 1 was followed by the E. A. Landreth discovery at Ibex in 1921 and the Cook Field in 1925, a prolific shallow field that marked its seventy-fifth year of operation in 2000.

One gets the impression that the courthouse may have become in disrepair toward the end of the nineteenth century and beginning of the twentieth century. Numerous comments were made concerning janitorial work. The court reprimanded the janitor, T. W. Hill, for permitting boys to assemble on top of the courthouse, breaking glass and vandalizing around the clock. Again, in 1914, the roof was repaired, and in the next year, the Ladies Civic League initiated trees being planted on the square and, at the ladies request, water piped to them. The ladies also asked the court to designate the northwest corner of the yard for a public park to be named Marshall Park for Sheriff Marshall Biggs. The court's response was that although it was a good idea, they had no authority to do this. Meanwhile, new toilets and closets were plumbed into the second floor along with a new septic tank. One would assume this was a convenience for the men. The same year the Texas Central Railway Company sold out and became part of the Missouri, Kansas, and Texas Railway Company, better known by the nickname of the "Katy."

Once again smallpox struck. This time it occurred in Moran where a quarantine was placed around the town and surrounding area to prevent its spread. This epidemic was not nearly as severe as the earlier one in 1882.

Some mention of floor repair and replacement in the courthouse are made in the minutes of 1910, 1918, and 1937. However, it is unclear when the oak flooring was laid down over the original pine floors other than being done in a piecemeal fashion. For example, the original floors in the clerk's office were removed in 1910, Judge Dyess was ordered to have the floors repaired in the clerk's office in 1918, and oak flooring was installed in the home demonstration agent's office in 1937. Perhaps the use of coal stoves in the early years had damaged the flooring and necessitated the repairs and replacements. Closets to be used for storage were placed under the first floor stairways in 1919. Whether or not the stairways were altered and balusters removed at that time is also unknown. A more ornate group was located in attic storage just in time for the restoration of the building.

One hundred sixty two citizens led by A. W. Reynolds, father of the late Alice Reynolds—Albany artist and musician who designed costumes, wrote music, and played the organ for the *Fort Griffin Fandangle*—presented a petition asking the court "to repair the County Courthouse and beautify the same by the construction of concrete sidewalks and curbing around the square and concrete sidewalks to each entrance of the building, doing any work that may be necessary for the beautifying and improving the Courthouse and the Courthouse grounds." The architectural plans and specifications for such work were to be done by S. J. Churchill for seventy-five dollars. This was accomplished in stages over the next three years. New chairs were purchased for the county and district court rooms to replace those broken and useless.

53

In 1920, William Kenshalo and eight members of the Guy Taylor Post of the American Legion of Albany introduced a petition to the court. It requested space on the southwest corner of the courthouse square to build a structure dedicated to the memory of the Shackelford County boys "who gave their lives and their services for the protection of humanity in the Great War that has just closed and for the use of all ex-servicemen in said war." The court agreed to the proposal, but the structure was never built although a cannon was placed on the northwest corner as a memorial. Except for the 1926 jail on the northeast corner of the square, it has remained unencumbered by superfluous buildings, enhancing the attractiveness of the courthouse itself.

The Albany News reported in early 1921 that "a large force of hands are cleaning up the Public Square. That old shang-high iron fence which has been an eye sore for fifteen or twenty years has been torn down and moved away. . . . All old rubbish, the accumulation of years, is being removed and those shaggy trees are being trimmed up. These old hitching posts have been taken up and moved further out. . . . When they get through with the job, it is going to look spic and span. Of course this is just the beginning on the public square; eventually it is going to be made a beauty spot, when the plans are finally finished as drawn. On account of insufficient funds, the county is going to do the work by peace meals [sic], but . . . by next year they will be able to finish it up as outlined by Messrs. Proctor Clarke and Sheriff W. M. Biggs."

After the "old shang-high iron fence" was discarded, stock began grazing on the lawn once again. For years a section of that fence could be seen along the

CIRCA 1911

County Judge J.A. King with typists

54

front of the lawn at the Bob Nail House across the street from the courthouse—now the "Old Nail House" a bed and breakfast. Every year at *Fandangle* time a row of white daisies dramatically bloomed on the street side of the fence.

To prevent the animals from taking over, bids were taken for surfacing the square, and Roy Matthews was hired at fifty cents per cubic yard. Penick-Hughes of Stamford did the "piping for the Courthouse square" for $62.16, but before the work could be finished, the courthouse caught fire in 1922. The court minutes reflect their anxiety. "The Shackelford County Courthouse caught fire, and for a brief time it seemed that the entire building would be destroyed, thereby entailing a great loss in property and civic beauty to the entire county." The fire started in the clerk's office.

The Fire Department removed furniture, fixtures, and records saving all without any great loss. The Moberley boy was injured while fighting the fire and the county paid his medical expenses. As a result, the county purchased additional insurance with Webb & Hill from $31,000 to $50,000 on the building, from $1,600 to $5,000 on furniture, fixtures, clock and library, and bought hail and tornado coverage for $20,000. They also asked for more water pressure in the alley pipe line south of the courthouse. The repair was done by O. V. Lemmons for $5,060 and included a metal ceiling installed in the district courtroom, but did not include the floor in the southeast witness room and surveyor's office.

Painting was done by J. C. Parnell and wiring by L. S. Hollowell. After the square was cleaned and finished, the Girl Scouts asked for and received permission to erect a small building on the northeast corner of the square for a library and a rest room at no cost to the county. If it was ever built, it is long since gone. During the restoration, signs of the old fire still remain on the district courtroom rafters. Since the county immediately advertised to "wire for electrical purposes" after the fire, perhaps the gas lighting or equipment was involved in the incident.

Oil discovery in 1926 led to a new economic era for Shackelford County. At a depth of only 1,241 feet, an amazing shallow oil formation now known as the Cook Field was found on the W. I. Cook Ranch five miles northwest of Albany. This abundant production made several fortunes and built the W. I. Cook Children's Hospital in Fort Worth. It also prompted county improvements— courthouse painting, a parking lot with access to the east entrance, and a new jail. Bailey, Burns, & Fitzpatrick of Dallas built the first additional permanent structure on the northeast corner of the square out of Lueders stone and concrete for a cost of $39,500. The plans were drawn by the Pauly Jail Building Company of St. Louis, Missouri but with County Judge Richard T. Dyess very much in charge. Out-of-doors plumbing was still a necessity. The court erected a stone outdoor toilet. Perhaps the men working on the jail required its construction, but it was placed near the courthouse. The lack of a fence continued to pose dilemmas. The court set a fine of five dollars on persons who make public paths on the courthouse square.

The upcoming Texas Centennial prompted many to think about the past and the accomplishments worthy of honoring. Judge J. A. Matthews, one of the few survivors of the pioneer trail drivers, chose to make a fitting memorial to the trail drivers and place it on the courthouse lawn. Made of metal, the shaft is surmounted by a longhorn steer with a small caption below to commemorate the "Texas Cattle Trail to Dodge City, Kansas and other Northern Points, 1875–1890." At that time, *The News* remarked that the trail generally was called the Fort Griffin—Dodge City Trail. Today, historians properly refer to it as the Western Cattle Trail. Nearly a half million cattle, jacks, and horses passed over the trail in the period of 1880-81. Appropriate dedication ceremonies recognized these men listed in *The News* in addition to Judge Matthews: P. W. Reynolds, Bud Pate, George Pate, Jesse Pate, Charles Kenshalo, Jerry Hollis, Louis Shoffit, Sr., T. J. Matthews, and Bill "Tige" Avery, colored. The newspaper apologized for any names left off the list.

Judge J. A. "Bud" Matthews was husband to Sallie Reynolds Matthews and father of nine children including four who lived in Albany or used it as the center of their operations. Descendants of Joe B., Ethel, Suzette, Sallie and May still live in Albany and contribute to county life. Watt remained unmarried

55

throughout his ninety-eight years. In *Interwoven* Sallie commented on her husband's political undertakings. The Lambshead Ranch is mostly in Throckmorton County, and right after the county organized in 1879, the Judge served as a county commissioner in the new county only twelve miles away. Three years later, the Matthews moved back to Albany where they already had a home. In 1894, he told the family that he was going to run for County Judge of Shackelford County. When asked by his wife why he wanted to do that, he replied that he wanted to get rid of the nickname, "Bud." He was elected and did serve for two terms and thence was called Judge, having forever lost the nickname he had had since boyhood. Judge Matthews' grandchildren living in Albany today are John A. Matthews III; John H. Burns; Watt M. "Palo" Casey; Robert S. Brittingham; Ardon B. Judd, Jr.; and great-grandchildren Watt M. Casey, Jr.; Rodney L. Casey; David D. Casey; Sally Blanton Stapp; and Liz Blanton Green.

56

It is interesting to note that during the Great Depression Shackelford County had its largest population. The census recorded 6,695 population in 1930. This resulted because of increased oil and gas exploration and the success of the Cook Field.

Flush with new tax money and needing more space, the court contemplated an addition to the county clerk's office. The county hired Knight and McKelvy to secure plans and estimate a cost and seriously considered adding on to the courthouse in 1934, but the idea was shelved. Two years passed and the county made instead an important move to correct the chronic roof problem—a sixteen ounce cold-roll sheet copper roof was installed by Jim George, a local metal craftsman. George used the slogan, "Made in Albany, by George!" Copper is supposed to last up to 150 years, but the building expanded during the years, and the butt-welded seams popped apart and could not be repaired. In 1937, the clerk space problem came up again, and Fred Buford of Abilene was hired and proposed a solution of sealing off the south entrance thereby creating office space from the hall area. Two fire escapes were added on the south exterior facade, and at last a ladies toilet was placed in the building adjacent to the west storage closet under the stairways. J. D. Jones was paid $1,978 to execute Buford's plans plus $291 for the two fire escapes from Central Texas Iron Works.

In 1938, having returned home from schooling in the East, a young graduate of Princeton University, inspired by the recent Texas Centennial pageant, wrote *Dr. Shackelford's Paradise* as a senior play. Robert E. Nail, Jr., had spent a short time directing theater in Fort Worth before bringing home his Phi Beta Kappa key and an inherent love of young people to teach English in Albany High School. While at Princeton, Nail had made a name for himself writing plays in a class filled with notables. The senior production was so successful that spring, it was renamed *The Fort Griffin Fandangle*. Encouraged by high school superintendent

C. B. Downing and chamber of commerce manager Miss Ollie Clarke, it was presented again that summer by the town using all local talent. Nail also wrote the *Albany Nativity*. It is presented at no admission fee every other year at the Aztec Theater. Many Albany folks think this is Nail's best writing effort.

A mixture of song, dance, and narration, the *Fandangle* has brought wide acclaim to Albany. The historical pageant was held on the high school football field until all of the young men including the director went away to war. After the war, the production continued with Nail doing the directing and Alice Reynolds writing music, playing the organ, and helping with sets and designing costumes. The producer of the show was G. P. "Crutch" Crutchfield, a "can-do" type of fellow who, as an engineer with Marshall R. Young Oil Company, had access to the men and machinery it took to bring Bob Nail's *Fandangle* to life. He oversaw the construction of a steam calliope, stagecoach, and miniature train. Every other summer folks came from near and far to Albany to see the production based on the recollections of the Old Timer about "times long since dead." An assortment of costumes, flags, and props have been accumulated to use in the show. Over 250 local people of all ages took part in the production always held the last two weekends in June.

After Crutchfield's death, the production stalled for a number of years, and there was talk of moving it to Abilene. A young local man from a Shackelford County ranching heritage, Johnny Musselman, came home from the University of Texas with an offer to help. After holding one year's production on the Musselman Ranch southeast of town, Watt Matthews, who ran Lambshead Ranch on the Clear Fork, furnished a location near the old shipping pens at the northwest edge of town where the *Fandangle* could build its own amphitheater. Watt Matthews took over as an unofficial producer, furnishing horses, mules, buffalo, wagons or whatever it took to make the show go on. And the show did go on. With Katharyn Duff, columnist of the *Abilene Reporter News* and friend of Albany, cheering and supporting the show, twice the *Fandangle* cast presented shows at the LBJ Ranch at Johnson City, once while President Johnson entertained a group of Latin American diplomats. The *Fandangle* received notoriety, and the show was presented in a variety of towns and venues. The most important spring sampler went on at Lambshead Ranch each year for all members of the Fort Griffin Fandangle Association. Bob Nail suddenly suffered a heart attack in 1968 and died before he could be taken to the hospital. The whole town was grief stricken and wondered what would become of the production he had so lovingly nurtured.

After months of soul searching and planning the show kept going with leadership from those Nail had trained, and Watt did everything he could to support those who directed the show. Members of the Fandangle Association

57

Board of Directors bolstered everyone's efforts. Since his death, directors have included the late James Ball, a local talent who was an excellent songwriter and performer, the later Marge Sedwick Bray, best known as the Albany dance teacher and Bobby's choreographer, and Betsy Black Parsons who grew up in the show and was Marge's protégé. It continues to the present day, now led by those like Betsy and Louann George, current music director, who were children in Bobby's productions. When the show moved to the theater, the barbecues that had been held around town in various locations settled on the courthouse lawn where many of the 10,000 visitors who come each year eat their dinners before the show.

Shortly before his death, Joe Blanton confided that he had thought it was best for the courthouse when, in 1939, it was decided to remove the old wooden windows and install steel windows throughout the building "so as to prevent rain and dust from entering the rooms of the Courthouse." The old windows were in bad condition, but as Joe realized after years passed, steel wasn't the answer, either. Nevertheless, all concerned took action they thought would extend the building's life, and at a cost of $3,900 paid to Charles F. Williams of Fort Worth they were installed in all outside windows "except the belfry in the dome where the clock is situated." All were painted with two coats of paint, plaster repaired and woodwork and plaster painted with three coats.

Cattle rustling was not over, it seemed. In a spectacular case of the time, Bob Compton of Shackelford County was accused of cattle theft from H. W. Lee, a neighboring rancher. Compton had been tried in the Spring District Court term of 1939 and found guilty and sentenced to a two-year prison term. Dallas Scarborough of the Abilene firm of Scarborough and Ely, acting as defense counselors, won a reversal in the Court of Criminal Appeals in Austin. Harold Law still remembers the enormous crowds attending the trial.

In June 1940, invitations were sent throughout the state for the dedication of the Texas Company plaque and miniature oil derrick. The memorial had been given to the Albany Chamber of Commerce and they immediately started a movement to place it on the courthouse lawn to call attention to the oil operators who developed Shackelford County Oil and Gas. The principal speaker at the event was John Lee Smith of Throckmorton, and president of the chamber, J. Carter King, Jr., served as master of ceremonies. The celebration was broadcast over KRBC in Abilene.

Bob Nail purchased the old County Jail to house his collection of memorabilia. The popular *Dallas Morning News* columnist Frank Tolbert wrote about Bob Nail's Alphabet House, as he called it, because of the initials carved into the rock by the workmen. The initials were placed there at the time of construction so that the stone masons could be paid accordingly. Bob amassed a large collection of local photographs and diaries, scrapbooks, and family papers. Everyone entrusted him with their most precious belongings because they knew he would take care of them and keep them for historical purposes. Upon his death the building was converted to the Old Jail Art Center and Robert Nail Archives by his nephew Reilly Nail and his cousin Bill Bomar. A number of Albany citizens had primary roles in this effort including leaders from such families as the Jacobs, Jones, Young, Green, Hooker, and Stasney.

The Old Jail Art Center has received national acclaim, and the archives are more valuable than ever and have been added to by Joan Halford Farmer of Albany, long-time archivist and historian, and others interested in passing along historical material. Recently, some special collections have been added, such as that of Graham and Sam Webb.

One of the cherished treasures in the Old Jail is a Tonkawa doll given to Sallie Reynolds Matthews as a child and placed at the Jail by her younger son, Watt. An *Albany News* item in 1943 marked the death in Oklahoma of the last Fort Griffin Tonkawa, John Rush Buffalo, at the age of seventy years. He had been fourteen years old when he left Fort Griffin in 1884.

By 1941, the courthouse roof once again became a problem. Lydick Roofing Company of Abilene repaired it. The country was at war, and county folks did their part to contribute in a number of ways including collecting scrap metal. Contests took place as a way of stimulating friendly competition in the area. The West Texas Chamber of Commerce conducted one such contest that lasted two years, and in awarding the first place $400 check to Albany, President C. M.

59

CIRCA 1911

County Judge J.A. King's Office

Caldwell of Abilene enumerated quite an amazing list of contributions from the town accomplished between 1941 and 1943. These included several war bond drives that exceeded their quotas; scrap paper, metal, and rubber drives; sponsoring victory gardens in eight out of ten homes and processing 8,122 cans of food; maintaining a Red Cross production room that turned out 5,000 finished garments. Miss Ollie Clarke, I. M. Chism, and C. B. Downing accepted for the town. Albany's 1940 population stood at 2,234 people, but this is representative of the type of mobilized effort Americans were undertaking during World War II.

Shackelford County's young men joined the war in Europe and the Pacific. One of Albany's best-known war stories involved Judge Dyess's son Edwin Dyess. Born here in 1916, Ed received pilot's training at Randolph and Kelly fields in San Antonio after graduating from Albany High School and Tarleton State University. Edwin grew up around the courthouse during the ten years his father served as county judge. He went to the Pacific and was assigned as commander of all flying squadrons on Bataan in the Philipines. In Subic Bay, north of Manila, he alone destroyed enough Japanese ships to make the enemy think they had been attacked by a force of bombers and fighters.

In a short while, MacArthur left the Philipines and U. S. forces were compelled to surrender. Dyess refused to leave the island when he had the chance because there was not room for all of his men to leave. Consequently, he was captured and held in three prison camps for 361 days by the Japanese and subjected to inhumane treatment. The forced march from the point of capture to the first prisoner camp north across the length of the island, made without food or water, has been called the Bataan Death March, but Dyess survived. Ultimately, Dyess and several others escaped the third camp and with help from Filipino guerrillas linked up with American forces.

After recovery in an military hospital, Colonel Dyess returned to Albany on his way back to active duty. By that time, he was a full-fledged war hero. He spoke to hometown folks who packed the football stadium. In December 1943, he reported for active duty in California. While flying a P–38 Lightning, whose "dazzling speed always had fascinated him," he crashed and was killed. Albany was plunged into grief. No one could believe that the hometown boy who had endured so much could have come to such a tragic and sudden end. Five weeks later his story broke in *The Chicago Tribune*. He is buried in the Albany Cemetery, and in 1956, this highly decorated West Texan was memorialized by having Dyess Air Base in Abilene named for him.

These three people previously mentioned had productive lives in Albany. I. M. Chism was county judge for many years and deacon of the First Baptist Church, and Superintendent Downing seemed to be involved in all of the good things that happened while he was in Albany. Miss Ollie taught in the Albany schools, worked for fifteen years at the bank, and for over twenty years was manager of the Albany Chamber of Commerce. She accomplished many big things within the county. It was Miss Ollie who pushed for Fort Griffin to be made a state park; Miss Ollie promoted the park and swimming pool to the city council (which she talked the ranchers into paying for); and Miss Ollie encouraged Bob Nail to expand the idea and spirit of the *Fandangle* as part of Albany's summer life. She was the daughter of Mr. and Mrs. A. A. Clarke.

For the World War II home-front effort even the cannon placed on the square to commemorate World War I veterans was given up as scrap metal. Retired Lieutenant Colonel Ed Tackett came to Albany as a young child in 1931, but did not go into the courthouse until after the war when ordered to do so to file his discharge papers there. His early memories center around the square and the cannon. His recollections are that as a young child living only five blocks away, he went by himself to the "park" or playground on the southeast corner of the square where there were swings, a merry-go-round, a slide, locally made monkey bars, and "a few other items that were maintained in good condition."

61

Bob Green, rancher and historical writer, recalls that the equipment was moved to the courthouse lawn from Webb Park that was situated along the south side of what is now Breckenridge Street just east of the creek. Not being an air-conditioned world then, Tackett remembers, the "park," as it was referred to, provided "the coolest and most pleasant place in town on hot, still summer days." In the 1950s the park moved to the swimming pool area and is now called the City Park. The Webb and Andrew Howsley families sponsored this recreation and picnic area for the public. The Ledbetter Picket House was moved in from the banks of the Clear Fork and placed adjacent to the park and next to the city water works. Mr. Gray Webb moved in the old rock civil jail from the Flat.

Tackett remembers that the cannon was a gathering place for the male youth in the community. "Unless something big was happening at school or homework was demanding, the gathering started each evening after dinner and lasted until about nine o'clock. The early arrivals got the seats next to the barrel, the next two or three the barrel itself, and the late comers the wheels, the tongue, or wherever else they could locate." From this vantage point they could congregate and "enjoy a view of the goings on in the community." Social mores had very different themes from current times—no drugs, no vulgarity, no alcohol, and no smoking. The youths seemed to have been more interested in forging the friendships that served them well during World War II when they were called to fight for their country. Many of them were away in the war when the cannon was donated for scrap metal, and Tackett expresses regret over it being given.

After the war, the ones fortunate enough to return came back to wives or sweethearts and resumed their lives. A new bandstand, built in 1948 near the northwest corner of the courthouse square, became the site of open air concerts given by the Albany Band. *The News* comments:

> Albany is proud of her new bandstand and the United States flag that floats from it. Albany is not dead as some of her neighbors and even some of her citizens tried to think. She may have been a little lethargic for a while, but she is waking up from her lethargy to put on new life and drink in new vitality. Just watch Albany grow. On Friday night the Albany band treated the citizens to an open air concert on the court house lawn. The music was very fine and showed what a home band can do when it has energy and talent. The people of Albany appreciate very much the music which the band renders and are very proud of its possession. They trust that this form of entertainment will be repeated quite often. The band stand adds very much to the effectiveness of the music and speaks for the enterprise of the town.

The *Fandangle* began again and the trains still ran. Two young men J. B. Cauble and Marcell Smalley, just back from the war, were killed instantly when their small plane stalled and crashed at the Cook Field Camp in 1947. A double military service directed by Castleberry's Funeral Home was held on the courthouse square and attended by an estimated 1000 persons. Author and researcher Joan Farmer attended the service and recalls the beautiful hymns at the end of the service. The choir sang "Not now, But in the Coming Years," followed by the entire assembly singing, "Blest Be the Tie That Binds." The double burial was made in the Albany Cemetery.

The Albany Study Club under the leadership of Mrs. J. C. (Margaret) Putnam initiated the concept of having a county library in the courthouse. After a committee was appointed to study this, the club voted unanimously to operate a library for the county. Mrs. Putnam recalls that the commissioner's court agreed to allow a library in the building if the Club would be in charge, and says that a Book Tea held at the Methodist Church resulted in collecting 135 books to begin the project. That nucleus grew quickly. Two long-time librarians were Mrs. Bland (Elsa) Turner and Mrs. Jewel Lackey. In 1961, the library moved from the courthouse to the old Southwestern Bell Company's red brick building north of the downtown area. Today, the Albany Study Club and the county still have the same working arrangement.

Finally, in 1956 window air cooling units were put into the offices of the courthouse except for the courtroom that wasn't cooled until 1985. These units were evaporative coolers and not very effective.

No one in the courthouse realized the cumulative weight of the old records stored over the district courtroom until on June 5, 1958, when a 15 X 30 foot piece of metal ceiling collapsed scattering paper and trash all over the courtroom. County Attorney Matt Blanton left his office to enter the courtroom just as the ceiling came down, narrowly missing a serious accident. Miss Maxine Palm, secretary to Judge Chism, said the cave-in sounded like rocks tumbling. Staff writer for the *Abilene Reporter News*, Jim Eaton, commented that perhaps the building would not last 500 years after all.

The first impulse was to sweep everything up and haul it to the dump, but archivist and *Fandangle* director, Bob Nail, knew better. With help from some of the town's teenagers, he sorted and saved many important items including the original petition to organize the county that is in the Robert Nail Collection. Joan Farmer remembers helping to go through and sort the documents.

The repair involved Mauldin-Ballard and Associates, architects and engineers of San Angelo, designing a new lower ceiling of acoustical tile, and Rose Construction Co. of Abilene doing the work. Within a few months the ceiling had been repaired and "all chairs, jury rails, doors, floors and walls" had been repainted and the court decided the old window blinds needed to be replaced, too, at a cost of $274.20. A well-thought-of local engineer, Floyd M. Johnson, received $250 to inspect the work and verify its safety.

Following the lead of the Texas State Historical Survey Committee, the Shackelford County Committee wrote the commissioner's court concerning a medallion for the Courthouse. The court voted unanimously to purchase one and pay for it. Bob Nail was chairman of the Shackelford County Historical Survey Committee, and Joan Farmer was secretary.

When the *Fandangle* opened in 1965 in its new amphitheater given by Watt and built by local people with mostly volunteer labor, Bob Nail directed the show. Johnny Musselman served as producer, Alice Reynolds was music director, Chamber of Commerce Manager Winifred Waller directed ticket sales, and Donny Hardaway acted as stage manager. Bob Green and Marilynne Jacobs narrated the show, James Ball wrote four new songs including "Remember When" which was the theme of the show, and Clifton Caldwell and Arthur Dinsmoor did the lighting. Lead singers were Marilyn Martin, James Ball, Jon Rex Jones, Clifford Teinert, Richard Middlebrook, Gayla and Rita Townsend and Midge and Kathy Rodgers. Mack Eplen's of Abilene catered the Courthouse Barbecue for $1.25 a plate.

The last train did run when the Missouri, Kansas, and Texas Railway Co. discontinued the line in 1967 except for a small strip from Gorman to Dublin, saved to haul peanuts. For eighty-three years the tracks had been a central part of downtown Albany and a lifeline to Moran.

63

CIRCA 1942

COURT HOUSE ALBANY, TEX.

64

Governor Preston Smith came to the centennial celebration of Fort Griffin planned by Bob Nail and held at the Fort Griffin Campground. Two hundred people came to observe the one hundredth birthday. The county seat's one hundredth anniversary followed seven years later, and it was held on the courthouse square on September 14, 1974. A county fair commemorated the event with more than forty activities and entries. Sponsor of the affair was the Beta Sigma Phi Sorority and the highlight of the day focused on a historical marker dedication at the newly restored Henry C. Jacobs House. Special guests included Mr. and Mrs. Mark Meister and Mrs. Pauline Bellieu of Oklahoma City, Oklahoma, granddaughters of Jacobs, and Bob Watson of the Texas Historical Commission. A giant birthday cake with one hundred candles fed the guests and Miss Nell Sammons, Centennial Queen, was presented. An official county flag flew from the flagpole, the result of a contest sponsored by Lee's Legion Chapter of the DAR and won by Bobby Williams, a seventh grader in the Albany Public Schools.

At this time, the Shackelford County Historical Commission applied for National Register of Historic Places designation for the courthouse and selected surrounding buildings. As a result, in 1976 the courthouse and fifteen other buildings were named by the secretary of the interior as the Shackelford County Courthouse Historic District. The nearest similar district was at Granbury, Fredericksburg having been the first such district in Texas. Since 1976, one of the buildings has been lost. The Wilhelm House was torn down when the grocery store located on its lot and Albany preservationists could not talk Thrift Mart into using the small wonderful old building in their plans.

The idea of huge county celebrations continued when the Bicentennial of the United States was remembered with another county fair and dedication of an official Texas Historical Marker commemorating Shackelford County. At the same time the beautiful new gazebo designed by Albany native Van Jones was dedicated. The gazebo cost $8,000 and Robert Williams headed the building committee. Patriotic songs were sung by Clifford Teinert, accompanied by the Viertel Band. Bob Echols acted as emcee. Again a full slate of activities kept all ages busy, and the event provided fun-filled hours for a large crowd.

When the courthouse celebrated its one hundredth birthday in 1983, another crowd filled the square, delighted with Joe Blanton's booklet about the building's construction and clamoring for copies. That was the last large ceremony at the courthouse, until the Ray Seedig murder trial saw a crowded courtroom every day before he was found guilty of capital murder and sentenced to life in prison. Of course, the gazebo has been the setting for numerous weddings and several special meetings have been held there throughout the years.

In 1987 three women who were interested in Shackelford County history quietly formed the "Friends of the Courthouse" to work with the commissioner's court concerning improvements needed at the courthouse. These three were Dee (Mrs. Robert) Hamilton, Joan (Mrs. L. E.) Farmer, and Shirley (Mrs. Clifton) Caldwell. In 1995, seeking help for the leaking roof, the friends applied for Texas Department of Transportation enhancement funds (ISTEA) after having been turned down two years earlier. These were federal funds passed to the states to make local improvements along the highways, including historic buildings and sites. This time the application was successful, and the courthouse received $123,200 to replace the copper roof. The project was expanded to include restoring the clock tower, and the county received a $15,000 grant to complete the work from the Texas Historical Commission and its Preservation Fund. On May 4, 2000, in San Antonio, Texas, the Shackelford County Courthouse received $1,765,440 from the Texas Historical Commission and the Courthouse Preservation Program of the State of Texas.

Eight county citizens deserve a big thank you from all of us for funding the county's match for the grant received from the State of Texas through the Texas Historical Commission, making possible the beautiful results. These folks are A. V. and Pat Jones, Chuck and Marcia Jacobs, Jon Rex and Ann Jones, and Clifford and Lynne Teinert.

Today, a dream has come true. Due to the far-sightedness of then Governor Bush, Lieutenant Governor Perry, Speaker Pete Laney and the Texas Legislature, finally the total restoration is a reality. Stories like this are forever preserved, and Mr. Sinclair's prediction inches closer to realization.

CIRCA 1922

2 Our Courthouse

by Bob Green

CAN BUILDINGS HAVE AN EFFECT on the lives of people who conceive, erect and are in close association with them? Evidently they do for it appears that all down through man's history, he has constructed edifices to try and reflect his aspirations. The Parthenon, in Athens, Greece, now thousands of years old and crumbling, yet still is able to reflect the intellectual glory that so motivated the rise of Greek and Western Civilizations. The heaven-seeking spires of great cathedrals of Europe still bespeak of the intense religious fervor that possessed ordinary people of the Middle Ages and caused them to drop everything and engage in furious building programs of huge churches.

For us today the soaring skyscrapers of Wall Street and many other metropolitan areas are an everyday visual reminder of the tremendous power that money holds over our modern society. The edifices of men might give an insight to the ethos of those who build them. To pursue this line of reasoning closer to home, we might consider the circumstances of the building of our own Shackelford County Courthouse of which we are so justly proud.

The earliest pre-Civil War Anglo pioneers in this region lived in a turbulent, dangerous period. Struggling to exist on the very cutting edge of the West Texas frontier, far from civilized areas, they suffered from Indian depredations and hooligan lawlessness, yet never lost their dream of establishing a new order of life in the new country.

After the Civil War, the first community of this area was the civilian town of Fort Griffin. It was famous and even some of its more raucous citizens actually took pride in being known as "the wildest town on the prairie." Actually, that was true, for law and order in the town of Fort Griffin for all practical purposes was non-existent. That was much to the liking of a large part of its citizenry. For the flamboyant, bullying gunmen, professional gamblers, prostitutes, saloonkeepers and the dregs and losers of society back East who had drifted to the West, law and order were the last two things they desired. Unchecked licensciousness was really what they craved.

Yet, out in the countryside and even in the hell-raising town of Fort Griffin, there was another segment of society that consisted of God-fearing, family-oriented people who were seeking a place to put down roots and make a home in this new country. These were tough-fibered people who, practically on their own, had fought off and withstood the Indian menace and survived the rigors of harsh frontier living conditions. They were not to be intimidated by the thuggery of Fort Griffin. They were determined to start, in this new country, a just society based on the Christian, civilized values in which they believed. They wanted a town that reflected those beliefs, a town of law and order with schools and churches instead of gambling dens, brothels and a lack of morality.

This group organized, and in a close election held in 1874, won out over the lawless element of Fort Griffin. They voted to move the county seat of Shackelford County away from Fort Griffin to a new town called Albany some sixteen miles south near the center of the newly formed county.

Soon, in Albany, a simple picket-type building was erected in the center of a large square to serve as the new county's courthouse. But the vision of replacing that simple picket building with a far grander permanent structure of stone prevailed and became paramount. A building was wanted whose appearance would reflect and prove to all that the days of debauchery, corruption and lawlessness as practiced by the ruffians who ruled in Fort Griffin were over and would no longer be tolerated by the citizens of Shackelford County.

That they succeeded in doing so soon became apparent as their dream of a new courthouse became a reality. The old picket courthouse was moved off and a grand new one was started in the center of the square. This new courthouse would be built of enduring native limestone gathered off the scarps of nearby hills. When completed, it would be as strong as the strength of its builders' convictions. Today, well over a hundred years later, every plumb and straight line of the courthouse's rock walls still bespeaks to viewers the intentions its builders wished to project: that the structure represents a society of a people who want to live their lives under the rules of law and order. A decent society of God-fearing people, with good schools and churches. A society of citizenry living peacefully and in friendly harmony with each other, and sharing pride in their community. Today, this building still proudly stands for those same principles. It also stands as a fitting monument for those who conceived and built it. It is a monument to their faith in themselves and their hopes and aspirations for the town and county.

So, you could say that our courthouse, even like the Parthenon, really does exhibit the ethos of the men who built it, the early citizens of Shackelford County. They were a breed of men searching for a higher plane in life. Tough men, willing to stand fast and fight for what they truly believed was right, as God, who they never doubted was real, had given them the reasoning power to determine what was right.

Perhaps in an increasingly complex and rapidly changing world, this building will serve as a beacon to remind future generations that some dogmas never change. Such dogmas as the universal struggle between good and evil, between innocence and guilt, right and wrong. Choices must be made concerning these issues. Choices that others have made before us have led to our inheriting the finest form of government the world has yet seen. This government begins right here at home in the grassroots of courthouses and county administrations. Our political system has been passed down to us from predecessors who fought and even died that we might have it. It is a precious gift, and one that should not be taken for granted. It is a gift whose full value may never really be appreciated.

This refurbished building represents not only the hope for a better future, but also remains a symbol of the pride we maintain for our past. This is a good combination and one that Bob Nail expressed best for all of us in Albany when he wrote these words for the narration of his *Fandangle*:

We cherish that old building and its clock. It kept time for our fathers and grandfathers. As it measures our lives, it ties us to the past, that past which is long gone, yet not so far from us ever. There are trees still standing, that grew, young saplings then, on the riverbanks where the Indians passed. There are rocks on the hills that the iron tires of the Butterfield Stage cut with ruts. There are roads into town that the first white men, soldiers and hunters blazed on the unmarred prairie. There are chimneys still standing that the settlers first raised. Oh yes, the past is always with us. Read it in the weathered face of that old clock or hear it as it haunts the memories of old timers. Listen closely and hold it clearly in your head, these tales of past times. These stories the old timers have told. It is your heritage. If you remember, taking them into your heart to keep, then they will never die.

3 Congressman
Thomas L. Blanton & Sons

by Bob Green

THE SHACKELFORD COUNTY COURTHOUSE has had many colorful characters grace its halls through the years, but one of the most outstanding was Congressman Thomas L. Blanton. He started his law career in Albany, was elevated to be a District Judge, served over twenty years in Washington, D.C. in the House of Representatives and ended his career back where he started, in Albany, as a practicing lawyer in the courthouse.

Thomas L. Blanton was born in 1872 in Houston, Texas. His parents died when he was ten years old and he was reared by his grandparents in La Grange, Texas. As a lad he was up at 4:00 A.M., milked ten to fifteen cows, hitched up a team to a wagon and delivered milk to his milk-route customers. Early on, after milking the cows and while delivering milk before dawn, he was struck by the logic that a good education was necessary to accomplish what he wanted to do with his life.

After high school, he moved to Austin and got a job working in a mercantile store. When the bookkeeper died, he took over that job and earned every penny of his expenses at the University of Texas. He graduated from law school in 1897.

He was related to Sam Webb, an Albany banker who instigated his moving to Albany and opening a law office.

He soon married May Matthews, the eldest daughter of Judge J. A. and Sallie Matthews, and Watt Matthews eldest sister.

After several years of law practice, in 1908 he ran for District Judge of the Forty-second Judicial District against a much older but popular incumbent. Blanton showed his political skill in campaigning. He central theme was sobriety and youth. In the debates, he repeatedly mentioned his age (thirty-six) and insisted that the voters needed to elect a young, sober, non-drinking man. He made no direct accusation, but strongly implied his elderly opponent was not a teetotaller. Blanton won handily.

Politics, he found, was his element. He enjoyed his power as a judge, and maintained firm control of his courtroom at all times, often to the dismay of egotistical lawyers. He rode herd on them unmercifully, once fining one ten dollars for repeatedly standing in front of a lady in the courtroom audience. Although he offended many lawyers in his court, making some of them enemies for life, the public loved his dynamic personality and enjoyed his debating skills.

In 1916 he ran for and was elected Congressman of the Sixteenth Congressional District, which then ran from Mineral Wells to El Paso and was called the Jumbo District. From 1917 until 1937 he was a member of the House of Representatives where he spent his energy in Washington, D.C. fighting things he did not like, mainly organized labor, communism and liquor. Innately combative, his modus operandi consisted mainly of attack. His independent spirit as a self made man who had pulled himself up by his own efforts, made him an arch foe of organized labor, which he considered to be full of anarchists, communists and mafia-like thugs.

Samuel Gompers, then head of the A F of L became the center of his criticism. Blanton tried repeatedly to get anti-union legislation passed during his tenure in congress. This feud with Gompers lasted for years with Blanton claiming that union money was consistently sent to Texas to try and defeat him. This was true, but worse than that there was actual violence employed by union goons to try to intimidate him. One day a shot was fired at his car by a hidden assailant. The bullet entered through the windshield and exited the back window, passing through the car filled with his family. Miraculously, no one was hit. But Blanton didn't scare. As the feud continued, the fiery congressman's position was placed in jeopardy when he caused to be printed in the Congressional Record "grossly indecent and obscene language." The remarks were those made by a labor leader and Blanton was trying to show what mean people they were, but his enemies used this as a pretext to try and silence him. Today such language is heard daily on television, but in that more prudish time it was considered to be outside the pale. The House formally censured Blanton, but he steadfastly refused to apologize. Instead, according to one reporter, he made a stem-winding speech in his own defense, managing somehow to compare himself to both William Shakespeare and the heroes of the Alamo. He used this censure to his advantage back home with the voters as he pointed out it showed how much the labor movement hated him. The people in his district agreed and supported him vigorously.

Blanton was truly a scrapper, not only with words, but also occasionally with his fists. One fight occurred at a hearing when Congressman Bloom of New York, who was not a member of the convening committee, insisted on speaking anyway. Blanton, who was a committee member, took offense and the fight was on. No one was hurt, but Bloom's glasses were broken.

It seemed Blanton had trouble getting along with New York politicians. In 1935 he threatened on the floor of the House to thrash Representative Dickstein of New York to the point that "his own mother wouldn't recognize him." Blanton never backed down from a confrontation, was always ready for a fight and really appeared to love one. He was a scrapper.

Blanton now became known as "The Watchdog of the Treasury" and his opposition to spending bills enraged many of his colleagues. He bitterly fought against a proposal to raise congressmen's salaries, which brought him more enmity from his brethren in Washington. That didn't bother him one whit. He even rubbed salt in their wounds by introducing bills to reduce the size of Congress and to eliminate their travel allowances to save money. Irate congressmen defeated both bills. When those bills failed to pass, he attacked the fringe benefits of congressmen, such as their restaurants, barber shops, masseurs, which he contemptuously called "body rubbers," manicurists, and high priced chefs. Not all of this was political window dressing. Due to his environment and upbringing, Blanton was frugal by nature. In his eyes such extravagances that used taxpayer money was insupportable. There was one expenditure he always agreed on though, and that was any measure that would benefit ex-servicemen. He was a friend to veterans all his life.

In 1936 Blanton was defeated for reelection to Congress. Times had changed, people had changed and now had became more receptive to bigger government. A younger generation was ready for a change in their representation. They had grown tired of Blanton's fire and rancor and believed another more placid man could get them more largesse from a government that was now offering more and more services to people.

After his defeat Blanton returned to Albany in 1938, opened a law office and again practiced law in the old courthouse where he had started. True to form, he practiced with gusto. He would take any case, big or small, and fight vigorously for his client with his usual aggressive style. Some cases became classic. There was one where a steer had been killed by having its neck broken by the arm of a revolving pump-jack pumping oil. Blanton defended the oil oper-

73

ator by arguing that the steer was suffering from deep depression and had know-
ingly committed suicide to get out of its misery by sticking its head in where it
shouldn't.

Young lawyers beginning their legal careers with court cases in Albany
received quite an education when they came up against Thomas L. Blanton. A
young Breckenridge lawyer who eventually became a partner in one of Fort
Worth's top law firms never forgot how hard as a fledgling he had worked on his
first brief to be presented in the Albany courtroom where he was opposed by
Blanton. Many years later he still shook his head in disbelief in telling how
Blanton had made his opening statement, and then folded up his coat, and using
it as a pillow, proceeded to curl up on a table and go sound asleep. The sight of
the sleeping Blanton completely demoralized the young attorney, who felt certain that his carefully prepared brief must be inadequate if the opposing lawyer
felt so confident that he could sleep through his presentation. He also felt it
didn't help matters at all that the judge was so intimidated by Blanton he allowed such conduct in his court.

Blanton had raised four sons and a daughter. Due to his belief in higher
education, all four sons graduated from Princeton University. Three became lawyers, and at one time, all lived in Albany. The courthouse now became a Blanton
family stronghold with one son, Bill, the county judge, Tom, Jr., the county
attorney and their father, Thomas L. was almost the lawyer-in-residence. In one
memorable case the elder Blanton was a defendant's lawyer before his son's—
Judge Bill Blanton—court. Another son, Tom, Jr., was the prosecuting County
Attorney. Thomas L, Sr., true to form, became noisily bellicose in his argument.
Tom, Jr., objected strenuously about their father's histrionics to his brother, the
Judge. Judge Bill Blanton rapped his gavel several times and mildly admonished
the fuming elderly Blanton by saying, "Now simmer down, Dad, simmer down."

Years later, another son, Matthews Blanton, or Matt, would serve as the
Shackelford County Attorney for many years. Matt was a much respected and
even beloved county official whose efforts through the years in behalf of Shackelford County citizens were legion.

Although there are still Blantons in Albany, the fiery, hard-charging congressman and his lawyer sons are all gone now. But for us who remember them,
it is easy to imagine that the old courtroom still seems to reflect the powerful
impact of their strong personalities.

74

4 Sheriff Marshall Biggs and Rassie

by Bob Green 75

SURELY ONE OF THE MORE FLAMBOYANT, attractive personages to have ever served as an officer in the Shackelford
County Courthouse was the dapper Sheriff Marshall Biggs.
A man of many talents, early day pictures show him as a
member of an orchestra posing on the courthouse steps.
He played the cello. Another picture shows him in his courthouse office, boots on desk, cowboy hat pushed back on
his head, a sly look on his face, as he smilingly looks at the
camera out of the corners of his eyes. A large shaggy dog
is snoozing contentedly on the floor behind his chair near
a pot-bellied wood-burning stove whose stovepipe goes up
a way, and then turns sideways across the entire room to a
flue opening in the wall. It looks like a picture of a confident lawman who knows his stuff, and from all accounts
of those who knew him, that would be true.

Marshall Biggs was a popular sheriff who knew the
citizens of Albany and their idiosyncrasies very well indeed. Besides playing cello in the town orchestra, he um-
pired town baseball games, boldly entered into all civic
affairs, and was an adroit lawman who could handle hard
cases with force when necessary. He was, according to accounts of old timers who knew him, an all-around o.k.,
stand up guy. He was well known in the area and liked by
all, most especially the ladies, according to rumor. That is

76

believable for his pictures show him to be a handsome fellow indeed. Marshall Biggs was well ahead of my time, but growing up I heard my elders speak of him often with respect.

One of my favorite Marshall Biggs stories was told to me years ago by an older neighbor who knew him well. It seems baseball had become very popular just before World War I with all the surrounding towns having community teams during Marshall Biggs' tenure as sheriff. Competition between the teams of neighboring towns was fierce. Albany had a winning team mainly due to the incredible talent of its pitcher, who, to all accounts, would have easily made the majors today. His name was Rassie and he was good. Rassie also liked to drink, as well as play baseball and sometimes that habit got him in trouble. Like the night he and a friend had been up to no good, having availed themselves of someone else's whiskey and drinking until they were feeling exuberant.

Earlier that day, Rassie had helped unload some freight off a Texas Central train, placing all types of merchandise inside the depot. One of the items was a barrel of whiskey that had been ordered by an Albany saloon. Rassie had personally placed this barrel snuggly in a corner of the depot storage room. Later that night he and his friend returned to the depot, crawled beneath the floor of the storage room and carefully figuring out their position, proceeded to bore a hole with a brace and bit up through the floor boards with a large diameter bit. That successfully done, he changed to a smaller bit and now proceeded to pierce the bottom of the oak wood whiskey barrel itself.

His calculations beneath the floor as to where to drill had proved to be accurate and now upon removing the smaller drill, he was rewarded with a solid stream of Kentucky's finest whiskey which his friend carefully caught in an old dishpan he had thoughtfully brought along. Rassie hastily inserted a short piece of pipe of the proper diameter through the first large hole he had drilled in the floor and into the smaller hole in the bottom of the whiskey barrel. This short piece of pipe fit into the hole in the barrel bottom tightly, and as Rassie had put a cork in the lower end of the pipe, the flow of whiskey was shut off completely, but not for long. They had brought along two large, empty tin cans which they now proceeded to carefully fill by removing the cork from the end of the pipe. That done, the cork was replaced tightly to await another visit, and the two crawled out from under the depot and walked south down the alley that ran behind the row of buildings on the west side of Main Street.

Behind the Sackett House Hotel, they sat down in the alley and proceeded to empty the two cans of whiskey where it would do the most good, that being down their respective gullets. After enjoying the contents of the cans, burping and smiling, the two proceeded to weave across the street behind the bank and on down the alley toward home two blocks west of the courthouse.

As they passed behind a grocery store, they had to avoid a pile of old produce the grocer had discarded in the alley to be hauled off. As they stepped around the refuse, they passed close to a lighted window in the back of Lowery's, a men's clothing store, and peering in, saw the owner, a rather small, bald headed man, sitting on a stool before a high desk carefully entering figures into a ledger. The two stared in the open screenless window at the clothier who was engrossed in his accounting.

"Rassie," whispered his friend, "I'll bet you can't take one of them old big rotten potatoes there and hit old Joe in the back of the head with it."

Rassie stared fixedly through the window for a spell and then whispered back very seriously, "I believe I'll just take that bet."

He then bent down and selected a big Idaho potato from the pile. After an elaborate and somewhat exaggerated classic windup of a big league pitcher, he powerfully unwound and let fly with his best fast ball pitch through the open window.

Like it had been shot out of a cannon, that potato streaked across the room and literally exploded on the back of Joe Lowery's bald head. The impact knocked him off his stool and put him sprawling on the floor. Rassie and friend now ran giggling down the alley as Joe began to scream loudly, "Help! Help! I've been shot!"

Several loungers were talking and smoking while sitting outside on the high curb of the sidewalk in front of the store. Among them was Sheriff Marshall Biggs. Upon hearing the screaming, they all jumped up and rushed inside the store. It did look bad. The back of Joe's head was plastered with a gray, watery mush. Joe, flat on the floor, reached back and gathered some of the mush off the back of his head and brought it around to look at it. His face contorted in horror at what he beheld.

"My God! I've been shot! Look! It's my brains," he screamed and everyone recoiled except Sheriff Marshall Biggs.

Joe had appeared to faint as the Sheriff knelt down, reached out and took some of the mess off the back of Joe's head in his hand, smelled it, then shook it off and smiling grimly said, "Joe, you ain't shot and you ain't dead. Somebody just hit you in the back of the head with a rotten potato through that back window there, and I only know one guy in town who can throw a potato that straight and that hard."

With that, Marshall Biggs arose, left the store and walked swiftly south down Main Street and after three blocks turned west one block and knocked loudly on the front door of a silent, dark house. No one came. He banged louder and longer and finally the door opened slightly, revealing Rassie's mother, in a robe with her hair in curlers, standing in the crack.

"Why, what is it Marshall?" asked Rassie's mother in a soft voice that intimated people were asleep in the house.

"I need to talk to Rassie, Mrs. Martin. Is he home?" asked Biggs.

"Why yes he's home, Marshall, but he's sound asleep in his room there," nodding her head toward a closed door.

"Pardon me, mam," said Biggs as he shoved the front door open, pushed the mother aside and rapidly strode across the room. He opened the bedroom door and walked over to the bed. Rassie was indeed in the bed, covers up to his chin, eyes closed. Marshall Biggs stared down at the apparently sleeping man, then reached down and slowly drew the covers down, revealing a fully clothed Rassie, whose face slowly twisted into a big grin as he opened one eye, and said, "Reckon you got me, Marshall."

The long dead neighbor who told me this story vouched that he knew it to be true because he was one of the sidewalk loungers who, along with Biggs, heard Joe's screams and rushed to his aid. He also worked at the depot and the next day helped disconnect the whiskey barrel from Rassie's pipe and put a plug in the whiskey barrel. He finished the story by saying Marshall Biggs let Rassie out of jail in just a few days because Albany's baseball team was riding the train up to Lueders to play their team in a grudge match and they needed their best pitcher to pitch.

1959

5 Gene Richey and the Clock Tower

by Bob Green

GROWING UP IN ALBANY in the 1930s, the courthouse clock bell bonging out the time played an important part in my life as well as that of all my little chums. A classmate, and one of my best friends, was Gene Richey. Gene was an undersized but over-energized slip of a lad. He was as quick as a minnow with an adventurous spirit and sharp eyes that missed very little. One thing they hadn't missed was whispered excitedly to me in school one day. Gene had discovered that the door to the clock tower stairs on the third floor of the courthouse was not being locked, and the way was open for us to explore what lay up there beyond those steep tower stairs. It was the same urge of adventure that caused Columbus to discover America or Magellan to circle the globe. How could we refuse it?

So after school, we mounted our bicycles and zoomed down to the courthouse. We found the courthouse quiet, not much going on. We sauntered along the hall, looking in the open doors at busily typing women who looked up and smiled as we passed. We quickly sped up the stairs to the second floor and then on up to the third floor, which seemed to be completely empty of people. We approached the closed door that led to the tower stairs and grinned at each other as we saw the hasp that usually held the padlock that secured the secrets of the tower from interlopers was devoid of any lock. Our plan to explore was on go, and like Columbus passing the Azores, we opened the door, stepped inside and gently shut the door behind us. The die was cast; we had crossed the Rubicon into the unknown.

A musty smell assailed our nostrils, our little hearts beat faster and our eyes widened as we looked up the steep steps that were dimly lit by light filtering down the stairwell from above. It seemed to us we had now entered into an altogether different, almost mythic realm. Most exciting, though, was the loud, rhythmic clack-clack-clack-whir-whir-whir-rumble-rumble-rumble sounds from above, up the steep steps.

We cautiously crept up the stairs, the volume of noises increasing as we ascended. Upon reaching the top of the stairs, we entered into a small room with tall, elongated windows that seemed vaguely familiar. Orienting ourselves, we realized we were standing in the clock tower, just below the four clock faces.

82

A complicated looking boxy iron mechanism full of large and small cogwheels practically filled the room, and produced the loud, rhythmic clack-clack-clack sounds. We watched apprehensively as the largest cogwheel, which was slowly revolving, would be periodically stopped abruptly by a cam. This produced the loud clack sound. The cam would then retract, allowing the large cogwheel to revolve again, until the cam would advance and again stop it momentarily, producing another loud clack.

With a thrill to our boyish hearts, we realized we were actually in the midst of the almost magical clockworks that provided the correct time for all the citizens of the town. It was almost as if we were in the presence of and watching the beating of the open heart of Albany.

There was a large dressed stone weight suspended by a rope or cable that would slightly drop down lower with each clack. We were familiar enough with weight-driven grandfather clocks and cuckoo clocks to recognize that the weight of the large suspended stone, which probably weighed more than both of us together, served the same purpose in running this tremendous clockworks.

We wrinkled up our noses at a pungent but not unpleasant smell and realized it was coming from the oil that glistened and covered all the moving parts of the mechanism. A large oil can with a long spout sat on the floor. We carefully edged around all the clockworks until we were at the south side of the tower room where there was a ladder that went up to a small, rectangular open window. Up this ladder we scrambled and had no trouble slipping easily through the small window, out into the clear, pure fresh air of Shackelford County.

Now the clock tower has four large clock faces complete with hands four or five feet long and numerals large enough to see from the outskirts of town. A very large bell is just above in a cupola and strikes the hours and the half-hours in a very loud and determined fashion that can be heard all over town.

After going out the small window, we were very pleased to find ourselves on a small flat space directly over the south clock face. Above the clock face was a kind of convoluted framing that rose up a couple of feet and its frame. The space was just large enough for the two of us to sit side by side with our knees folded up and look out over the framing at the scene below.

Peering down to look at the clock face, we watched in amazement as the five foot long minute hand would jerk forward a little each time the clockwork inside went "clack." Then suddenly, all hell broke loose and our hair literally stood on end and we clutched each other wildly as, following a much louder whirring sound from the clockworks inside, came a tremendous clang from the big bell just over our heads in the cupola on top of the tower. Three more times the clangor of the bell rang out, the tremendous sounds seeming to make the whole tower shake, but, in our terror, it was probably just we who were shaking.

As the noise died away and we realized what had happened, we self-con-sciously turned loose of each other and Gene said sheepishly, but trying to act blasé, "Four o'clock. Set your watch." "Don't have one," I replied, still trembling a little. "Me neither," Gene answered and we grinned at each other, again as happy as two ten-year-olds could possibly be at our recovery from the unexpect-ed surprise of the cataclysmic striking of the town clock that had almost caused our nervous systems to short completely out.

From that day on, this place became our secret Mount Olympus to which, from time to time we would ascend to spend a most delightful hour or so in complete privacy, discussing our ten-year-old view of worldly things while look-ing down on the mere mortals below. But then, one fateful day, rushing up the courthouse stairs to the third floor after school, we found, to our dismay, that the hasp on the door of the tower stairs now boasted a brand new shiny padlock that was securely closed. Fate, or more likely the custodian, had intervened to bring an end to our courthouse tower escapade. Never again would we sit in our secret aerie over the south clock face. It was over.

But the effects of altitude may have caused a later development in Gene Richey. In a few years, he would enlist in the paratroopers and make three com-bat jumps in Europe during World War II with the Eighty-second Airborne Division. What was jumping out of an airplane after you had conquered the ledge over the south clock face of the courthouse?

Old Gene, after a long and successful career as a Federal District Attorney, has been gone for many years now, but still, once in a while when my gaze travels up to the south clock face of the courthouse, my aging eyes play tricks and I think I see two little blackhaired heads bobbing around up there like a couple of little crows in a nest, and I smile and think, Ah youth, what fun it was growing up in Albany in the 1930s.

1963

6 The Courthouse Recalled—A Memory

by Reilly Nail

MY SISTER MATILDA AND I spent our childhood or, maybe, formative years, living across the street from the courthouse, more properly known as The Shackelford County Courthouse. Our house was the small stucco one between the then and still imposing Hill House (now the Compton House) and our grandparent's large two story house (now the Old Nail House, Bed and Breakfast). The fact that the courthouse was an architectural gem and built in 1883 had no meaning for us. The courthouse was simply an extension of our yard and, therefore, gave us a far wider area in which to play. Actually, most of Albany was a play yard for children our age in the 1930s. A child could roam all over Albany with nothing untoward happening save for a skinned knee or, perhaps, some schoolboy scuffle. That both my sister and I are now over seventy, still alive and still almost kicking is proof of this fact. It also seems that genetically my sister and I were born climbers. In the back yard of our small house on now South Third Street—I don't think our street had a name then and it was unpaved—there was a big, fairly tall tree with many branches. Our house had a flat roof so very early on we began to climb to either the top of the tree or up and on the roof. Once, my sister, then about four, climbed up on the roof and, according to the late Margie Sedwick Bray, took off all her clothes. This prompted a telephone call from someone in the courthouse asking whomever answered in our house if they knew there was a naked young child on the roof! At this late date, I can only assume that my sister was dragged down from the roof and clothed. I also do not think it ever happened again.

By the age of seven and six, I being seven, Matilda being six, I am sure we had already discovered that the courthouse was full of endless possibilities for exploration, adventure, and even a secret club house. I do remember that it took us several attempts to discover the way up to the very top of the clock tower. One had to, first, enter the courthouse in view of all and nonchalantly climb the stairs to the third floor. Then, the adventure began. We took what we called secret passages, trap doors, and narrow spaces to emerge finally outside the clock itself and view all of Albany. Once outside and in full view, we could then wave and yell at those tiny figures below who were on Main Street. The choice times for visiting the courthouse tower were those times when the clock would chime the longest. The ideal time was either eleven or twelve noon. The sound would boom out and you had to cover your ears.

Our intimate knowledge of the courthouse was a great bonus for my sister and me in regards to friends our age who lived in Fort Worth. While Fort Worth offered a zoo, big, ornate movie theaters with real organs playing music and lights blinking, a huge train station, and, yes, Casa Manana, it did not offer a courthouse where you could climb to the very top. Consequently, the children of our parent's Fort Worth friends pleaded to make trips to Albany. Even today there are senior citizens living in Fort Worth who recall vividly their adventurous climb to the top of the Albany courthouse.

Still, we did have to be careful about when we did climb to the clock. If court was in session, then going to the top was out. A gang of young kids tramping through the hallowed halls of the court was frowned upon by everyone. We knew, most of the time, when court was in session because the windows would be open and voices could be heard even in the front yard of our house. Lawyers then orated in booming voices when before the court. One voice always stood out and we, when we asked whose voice is was, were told it was the voice of Judge Blanton. Although titled Judge, Judge Blanton was actually an attorney-at-law who frequently was before the court on behalf of a client. As it was, we knew nothing about what went on in a courtroom except there was a judge who sat in the high seat, a number of people inside the railing, and men with loud voices saying things to the judge and the other people. I do not think we even realized someone might go to the nearby jail as a result of an appearance in that courtroom. I do remember, however, my father going to the jail during that period to get someone out. Whom they were or what they had done, if I ever knew, is long forgotten.

As it was, the closest my sister and I ever came to actually being in the courtroom for a real reason was in June of 1938. It was during a *Fandangle* rehearsal on the football field in the early evening. My sister was in the *Fandangle* and I was just there as an observer. My uncle, Robert Nail, refused any plea of mine to be in the *Fandangle* on the grounds of nepotism. While I did look the word nepotism up in the dictionary, I was naif enough at that time to come away from Websters believing it referred only to males. I later found out my uncle really based his refusal on the grounds that I could not sing or dance. At any rate, that June evening the then sheriff and a deputy came across the football field and served my sister and me with a summons to appear before the court on such and such a date. We became instant celebrities that evening long before Andy Warhol ever mentioned his famous fifteen minutes of fame. That night, in many Albany households, the young singers and dancers gleefully told their parents, Reilly and Matilda were served with a summons by the sheriff and have to go to court!

Our charge was Removal of Disabilities of Minority which sounded very glamorous and promised courtroom scenes such as those we saw in movies at the Aztec. Now when the voices boomed out of the open windows of the courtroom, my sister and I would be the focus of these disembodied voices. There we would be, sitting in the witness stand, answering tricky questions from cunning lawyers. Alas, it was not to be.

Later, that same evening, the first cold water on our celebrity status and upcoming appearance in the courtroom was thrown by our grandmother, Etta Reilly Nail. "Don't be so excited about it," she told us firmly. "Its just something to do with one of those trusts the Nails are so fond of. Its really nothing but a formality." The next day, our father drove in from Fort Worth and extinguished any glowing embers that still existed. He informed us that Seth Barwise, a Fort Worth lawyer, was driving out to Albany to handle the matter and "you certainly don't have to appear in court." Matilda and I were crushed. Our big, anticipated moment in court vanished in seconds.

It was only some fifty odd years later that I finally did participate in a courtroom hearing in Albany's famous courthouse. I was a member of the jury in a trial that went on for a week. At the end of it, Judge Andrews told us, given the evidence and testimony presented, we could only find the defendant not guilty which we did. Some eight or nine years later I also sat in the public section of the courtroom to see a melodrama written by Bob Green and Pat Jones and put on a word processor by me. While I was happy to perform my civic duty as a juror and had a good time at the melodrama, these two occasions did not come anywhere close to the reality of being on the witness stand, raising my right hand, and swearing to tell the truth.

7 Dude Goes to Court

by Reilly Nail

WHILE MY SISTER'S and my one chance at a courtroom appearance in Albany's famous courthouse came to naught, my family, the Nails, have had some very close encounters with The Shackelford County Courthouse. My uncle, Robert Nail, was in the forefront of those fighting to save it when there was talk of modernizing it in the 1950s. I also know firsthand that when the ceiling collapsed around the same time, he was one of those who spent days sorting out the court records and entry journals littering the courtroom itself and various other offices below the ill-fated ceiling. I happened to be in Albany for some reason and was recruited to help. I was grateful then and still am for my uncle's participation in saving the magnificent 1883 building and the materials in there. I have since learned a great deal about its construction as the drawings for it by J. E. Flanders, its architect, now reside in The Old Jail Art Center housed in the 1877 limestone jail Robert Nail bought in 1940 in order to save it.

However, in the year of my birth, 1927, the then most prominent member of the Nail family and its defacto family manager, Missouri Matilda Nail Cook, spent a number of days in the august courthouse with a great many members of the Nail family by her side for support. From that time on until her death in February of 1932, Missouri Matilda Nail Cook could not look at the Shackelford County Courthouse without saying to whomever she was with and no matter how many times she had already said it to them before, "That building was where I spent one of the worst ordeals of my life!" (Throughout her life most of Missouri Matilda Nail Cook's sentences always seemed to end with an oral exclamation point whether called for or not.)

Missouri Matilda Nail was born in July of 1858 near Wolfe's Mill (later Wolfe City) in East Texas on land purchased from the State of Texas in 1849 by her grandfather, John M. Nail. At a very early age, she decided she hated her name, and her father, given to nicknames anyway, obliged by calling her "Dude." This nickname stuck and she was called Dude by her siblings the rest of her life. Her nieces and nephews called her Auntie as did the spouses of her brothers and sisters. In truth, the spouses of her brothers and sisters never enjoyed an easy relationship with Dude. In her iconoclastic view, her siblings' spouses were often the reason her siblings made errors in judgement, mistakes, or committed social gaffes such as drinking too much. The spouses, in turn, feeling much put upon anyway, happily adopted the term Auntie to call her. Auntie, they unanimously agreed, was a word, which to all outward appearances, sounded familial enough but in no way implied intimacy. In maturity, Dude was a large, imposing and dominating woman with a voice that alternated between sounding as if she was strangling or commanding a battalion. Even in her youth, she was a tall, large boned girl with a strong, dominant personality and, according to her brother, William Chapman "Buck" Nail, was born to rule. As it was, she did, indeed, rule the Nail family and many others from the age of seventeen until her death in 1932 at the age of seventy-four.

When still a girl she learned from her grandmother, Anna Watson Nail, that her grandfather had fled from Tennessee to evade the law. From that time on, as a third generation Texan and family manager, Dude's never-wavering goal was the gentrification of her Nail family. And from that same day on, she began laying down or inventing "Customs and Traditions" to which she demanded all of her family adhere. While never totally successful in bending her brothers and sisters and their offspring to living fully her often erratic list of Nail Customs and Traditions, Missouri Matilda Nail Cook's constant insistence had sufficient enough impact that, even today, the extant Nails at least pay lip service if not strict adherence to those precepts she set down.

In 1898, she and her husband, W. I. Cook, along with her brother, James H. Nail, visited Shackelford County for the first time. The Nail cattle operation, run by Brother Jim, had grown too large for the land available in Fannin and Hunt Counties and the land arrangements Jim had made for running cattle in the Indian Territory in Oklahoma were about to end. Albany and Shackelford County had been suggested to them as a promising new location for their cattle operation. Dude fell in love with Albany and the surrounding country at first sight and was the deciding factor in buying a ranch there. Once she had ridden around the Holstein Ranch on a horse, Dude exclaimed to Brother Jim, "The hills sing to me!" What she did not tell him, at that time, was she had also decided ranching should become a Custom and Tradition of the Nail family.

Dude, W. I. and Brother Jim bought the Holstein Ranch west of Albany on 1 April 1897. By December 1899, Brother Jim realized his sister and her husband were not ranchers in his definition of the word or, for that matter, were they ranchers in anyone else's definition either except their own. W. I. loved to hunt and fish and the appeal of owning a ranch in Shackelford County was the abundant opportunity Shackelford County offered to pursue what was supposed to be merely his pastime. As for Dude, to Brother Jim's consternation, her first concerns were not fences, tanks, or barns but refurbishing the original ranch house. Dude not only refurbished it from roof to cellar but staffed it with domestic help, and then kept it full of guests who had to be entertained. She also, to her brother's great annoyance, kept telling her guests that all the cattle they saw on the ranch were entitled to registration.

91

Finally, deciding enough was enough, in December of 1899, Jim offered to buy his sister and brother-in-law out. Dude immediately and adamantly refused. She was now convinced ranching was a Custom and Tradition of her Nail family and that was that. After 1898, one of her new mantras became that Granddaddy and Daddy really ranched but, of course, it was not called that in those days. Giving in, Jim sold his sister and brother-in-law his interest in the ranch and bought his own ranch, The Monroe Cattle Company Ranch, just across the north fence line. As soon as the papers were signed, Dude renamed her ranch The Cook Ranch. Brother Jim, not to be outdone, just as immediately renamed the Monroe Cattle Company ranch The Nail Ranch.

By 1912, after persistent persuasion, endless talking, and constant reminding that ranching was a Custom and Tradition of the Nails, Dude had uprooted three more of her siblings from their East Texas lives and brought them to Shackelford County. One sister, Rebecca Adeline Nail "Puss" Davis, reluctantly bought a ranch south of Albany in 1907 ostensibly for her son, Merrick. Later, however, when her flagship hotel, The Merrick, burned down in Paris, Texas, she, too, moved to Albany permanently. Brother Buck even more reluctantly bought the Lee Ranch west of Albany in 1910 and was living there when he died. Although both ranches are now owned by others, they are still known as The Merrick Davis Ranch and The Buck Nail Ranch. Her youngest brother, Robert, was the last, in 1912, to come to Albany but he opted for farm lands east of Albany rather than a ranch and a house in town. In 1913, Dude was able to boast proudly, Albany is surrounded by Nail ranches! In the spirit of full and truthful disclosure, her sister, Puss, and her brother, Buck, had other mitigating reasons for buying land elsewhere than East Texas but it was Dude's constant insistence that brought them to Albany and ringing it with Nail-owned land.

By the time Missouri Matilda Nail Cook moved to Albany, she had been a very imposing figure of a woman for some time. Very tall, ample of bosom, erect of posture, and always carefully and stylishly dressed, she resembled much more a patrician matriarch than the owner of a ranch west of Albany. She had lost her only child, a daughter and a grandson, in childbirth in 1901, a lasting tragic blow to her. In 1923, her husband, W. I. Cook, died unexpectedly of a heart attack leaving her a widow in all aspects of the word. With W. I.'s death, she decided to found something charitable in his and their daughter's memory. She finally decided on a charitable hospital to be built in Fort Worth and the first monies toward it were put into a foundation in 1925.

In spite of her and her husband's lack of acumen in ranching, The Cook Ranch was profitable thanks to their foreman, Talmadge Palmer. Missouri Matilda also had other sources of income from investments and her share from the sale of Nail assets in East Texas. Her husband, in spite of his lack of expertise in ranching, had an eye for investments and did very well with them prior to his death. Thus, it could rightly be said that Missouri Matilda Nail Cook was a woman of wealth in Texas of the 1920s. She did not drive so she was transported everywhere in a large robin's-egg blue sedan by Joe Thomas, a faithful servant of many years. (Joe Thomas was so faithful he even endured wearing a wool chauffeurs uniform during Texas summers.) She became one of Albany's sights, parking on Main Street, alighting from her large sedan helped by a chauffeur, visiting the various stores stylishly and immaculately dressed and walking with the aid of a gold headed cane.

Then, on 18 February 1926, Missouri Matilda Nail Cook's life changed radically. The first well of what, at that time, would turn out to be the largest shallow oil field in the world was discovered on The Cook Ranch. Missouri Matilda Nail Cook went from a woman of wealth to a very rich woman in a very short time.

With this discovery, *The Wall Street Journal* noted, "The entire history of oil in West Texas is changed." The more humorous locals of Albany equally noted, "With this discovery the entire history of the Nails changed too." As it was, the newly discovered Cook Field began the oil boom in Shackelford County and West Texas. Oil, as an economic factor, took root in Shackelford County and many fortunes were made because of it.

There is, of course, a difference in what in 1926 was considered very rich and what is considered very rich today. Still, no matter what the standard, there was a great deal of money involved, and in November of 1926 Missouri Matilda Nail Cook found there was a flip side to a sudden infusion of wealth. She was threatened with legal action over the placement of the south and east fence lines of her ranch. In March of 1927, she was driven to the Shackelford County Courthouse by the faithful Joe Thomas in a new Lincoln sedan—but still robin's -egg blue—where she marched up the stairs in a stately fashion to sit in the courtroom for the filing of *R. J. Moberley et al. versus M. M. Nail Cook et al., Boundary Dispute*. If this was not, as she termed it, enough of a cross to bear, she had to repeat the procession to the courthouse once more in June of 1927 when a similar suit, *W. P. Newell, Joe B. Matthews et al. versus M. M. Cook et al., Boundary Dispute* was filed.

As any of her brothers and sisters or her nephews and nieces would testify to, it was not a wise idea to rouse Missouri Matilda Nail Cook's ire. She was, by turns, stricken, visibly irate, and, in good Nail fashion, out for vengeance by these outrageous suits. After the June court session, she wrote in her journal as a note to her late husband, W. I., "They are making such an effort to take away part of the land you left me and by men you thought were your friends. I am hoping the Law will soon settle it and I will be out of this turmoil and my mind at rest and get out once more and listen to the cries of the birds and the sound of the hills singing."

93

The action brought by various individuals against M. M. Nail Cook and her fence line falls under the legal category of Adverse Possession. In such legal actions, the Defendant (in this case, M. M. Nail Cook) must prove she had enjoyed the use of the land under fence for a long enough time as to be hers and, furthermore, the original surveys confirmed the present land boundaries or were close enough to it. The plaintiff, on the other hand, had to prove M. M. Nail Cook had *not* enjoyed the use of land under fence long enough to be hers. In question was a strip of land at the south end of the Cook Ranch running east to west, 279 feet at its east end and 409 7/10 feet wide at its west end. In an area of Texas of extensive land holdings, this tiny bit of land seems somewhat frivolous to go to court over. The reason for it becomes clear when one realizes that on one side of the fence was the then worlds largest shallow oil field and on the other side there was not. By moving the fence line, the plaintiffs and their ranches would also enjoy the pleasures and profits of having part of the world's largest shallow oil field on *their* land too.

Dude was determined that "these robbing scheming so-called law suits where those vandals want to take away my land *is not* going to happen! As long as I have lungs to breathe and tongue to speak, I will let no one take this land away from me!" (This time her oral exclamation point is very valid.) Dude and her advisors began to prepare for these upcoming legal battles as one would prepare for going to war. For Missouri Matilda Nail Cook it was the absolute same thing. To that end, Dude and her brother, Robert E. Nail, Sr., assembled a group of lawyers that even in today's term of Dream Team would be impressive. Present in the courtroom of The Shackelford County Courthouse and representing M. M. Nail Cook, Defendant, in full force would be Judge W. R. Ely of Abilene (who now has a boulevard in that town named in his memory), The Honorable Joe H. Barwise and The Honorable Walter Morris of Fort Worth, Texas.

The plaintiffs, particularly, R. J. Moberley and W. P. Newell, became alarmed when Dude's defense team was announced and immediately began shopping around for more prestigious attorneys-at-law to represent them. However, since they did not as yet own a part of the world's largest shallow oil field, they were somewhat hampered financially in their ability to match Dude's defense team. Finally, they hired Goggans and Associates out of Dallas to plead their case. This, as it turned out, was a real mistake. R. J. Moberley, W. P. Newell and all connected to their side of the suit realized this on the first day of the trial, 28 November 1927. On that day, Judge Ely, an impressive figure of a man anyway, rose and declared, in his booming voice, to the court at large, "I was born in, loved, and know this country in dispute!" Such was the power of Judge Ely's voice that not only did the courtroom but everyone else in the courthouse learned what he knew, how he felt, what he thought. Hearing him was never a problem when Judge Ely was before the court. In addition, Judge Ely was already a name to be reckoned with in the legal world of Texas. His very presence in a court-room was rumored to awe both the jurors and the judge. No one connected with Goggans and Associates could make the same claim.

Furthermore, the plaintiffs' case was not helped in the least by the some-what dramatic arrival of Missouri Matilda Nail Cook in the courtroom at pre-cisely nine o'clock each morning of the trial. The large, imposing Dude literally swept into the courtroom, dressed stylishly for an outraged widow, even to a hat with a black veil pulled down to her chin, and using a gold headed cane. She was followed by an entourage of members of her Nail family who were there to offer a public view of stalwart and solid family support. What the others in the courtroom did not know was that the members of the Nail family, behind Dude's back, secretly drew lots as to who would appear in court that day as stalwart familial support. Dude would take a seat in the front row of the spectators' section of the court, fold her arms across her ample bosom and look straight ahead, looking neither right or left, during all the proceedings. In spite of look-ing neither left nor right, Dude somehow managed to convey to both the spec-tators and those on the other side of the bar exactly how she felt about any legal exchange taking place. Over the course of the trial, she managed to convey to all in the court, particularly the jurors, her outrage, affront, personal insult at the charges the lawyers for the plaintiffs were making. The plaintiffs and their families were no match for the theatrical display Dude and her family put on each day of the trial.

The major portion of the trial itself was very technical. In its transcript there are all sorts of allusions, references, and other legalese terms to varas, rock piles, mound marks, horseback chain surveying, and the like. It was a lawyer's dream to litigate and a layman's nightmare to explain. But the heart of the suit was whether a strip of oil rich land belonged to the Moberley and Newell Ranches or the Cook Ranch. Even today there are, in certain law libraries, still complete transcripts of, as it came to known, *Moberley et al. versus M. M. Nail Cook*. Until the advent of modern day technology, *Moberley et al. versus Cook* immediately became a landmark case in Adverse Possession suits. And, even though no longer valuable as a legal precedent, the trial is still sometimes used as a reminder of what once had to be proved in the bad old days before technology for the establishment of adverse possession.

Years later, in reading the transcript of the trial, it seems Dude's lawyers realized the trial itself was devoid of anything that touched on human emotions or human everyday understanding for that matter. Thus, in their closing arguments on 2 December 1927, it becomes very apparent that Dude's lawyers decided to intersperse what they felt were warm and touching glimpses of the defendant. The closing arguments are also replete with Dude's lawyers reminding the jurors numerous times what pain this trial has caused her.

Judge Ely led off the closing arguments for the defense in the same tone and voice he had used earlier in his opening arguments. His closing argument was once again heard throughout the courtroom and courthouse. He took great pains vocally to paint to the jury the picture of a little, defenseless, sweet old lady that these plaintiffs would throw off her land. The plaintiffs' lawyers, Judge Goggans and Associates, for some reason not disclosed, did not contest this statement and point out for the record the land in question was only 400 feet wide out of a 31 section ranch. Nor, does it seem, did the lawyers for the plaintiffs object to or the jurors, in deliberation, ever question the fact that a defenseless old lady about to be thrown off her land owned a chauffeur-driven limousine and was able to hire the best lawyers in Texas.

One would have loved to see the expressions on the faces of the plaintiffs and their lawyers when the Honorable Walter Morris rose to give the second in a series of closing arguments. In full voice, he began by telling the jury, "W. I. and Mrs. Cook, then young people, came to Shackelford County and bought this ranch in connection with James H. Nail for a consideration of forty-one thousand dollars. These good people, thirty years ago in this country, established their abode and bought that land and the deed says all of the land under fence.

95

They realized it would take a great deal of turmoil, strife, and hard work to meet their indebtedness. They lived there together, during all that time, striving and struggling, just as you gentlemen have strived and struggled to pay for the land you bought, I dare say, because I have done the same thing. They worked it during all of that time, struggling along, carrying water from the creek from which to prepare an evening meal. There was W. I. Cook working all day to meet his indebtedness, monarch of all he surveyed, coming home to meet his good wife who had carried water with which to prepare his evening meal. They were happy! No trouble came to them. And, by 1916, all the indebtedness was repaid."

No doubt Judge Goggans or one his associates as lawyers for the plaintiffs was very tempted to rebut the Honorable Walter Morris's statements by pointing out that W. I. and Dude were forty and thirty-nine respectively when they bought the ranch, not young people.

Equally, they could have rightly pointed out there was never any crushing indebtedness on the ranch at any time. And, had they a mind to, the lawyers for the plaintiffs could have quite rightly told the jury Mrs. Cook never carried a cupful, much less a bucket, of water from any creek to any house where she lived. Also that the nice evening meal the Honorable Walter Morris spoke so touchingly of was prepared by indoor servants who also cleaned the house and did the laundry. These same lawyers could have then closed their rebuttal by pointing out that, after 1916, Talmadge Palmer ran the ranch while Dude and W. I. wintered in Florida and summered in California.

One surmises the plaintiffs' attorneys, on hearing the first two closing arguments by the lawyers for the defendant realized the case was lost. If not, they then were certain when Judge Joe Barwise rose and announced in stentorian tones to the jury, "If the evidence does not warrant us in winning this lawsuit, all right, but, as Judge Ely put it, bring us in a verdict that can be framed and hung in the hospital that working girls may know a jury of Shackelford County would not take two or three hundred thousand dollars from them!" The jury did just that and the plaintiffs were ordered to go hence without a day and pay court costs.

From the perspective of some seventy-five years later, this suit may seem to be a bit silly and a lot of to-do over nothing. Yet, one must remember that this suit about to whom some three hundred acres of oil-rich land belonged was a gamble worth taking. Given the significance of the Cook Field discovery, these few hundred acres could produce over $500,000 in one year of 1927 dollars. The suit was a nice try by Moberley, Newell, and the others involved which came to naught. They duly paid the court costs and M. M. Nail Cook was able to declare, "God gave me the strength to sit in that courthouse all that time and hear and see all that was said and done by those vandals!"

Several days later Missouri Matilda Nail Cook received the following letter, framed it, and hung it in a prominent place on the wall of the living room of the Cook Ranch house.

> Moran, Texas, Dec. 3, 1927
> Dear Madame [sic]:
> I was the Fourman [sic] of the Jury in your recent law suit when the boundaries of your land was in dispute and I am glad to offer you at this time my hearty congratulations upon yur [sic] complete victory over your adversaries. I am not only glad, but real proud of the fact I was one of the jurors in this case to decide in yur favor for I was fully convinced from the testimony that this law suit was not only unreasonable but entirely unjust from the opponents side and I sincerely hope that the decission [sic] of this jury will discourage any further law suits of this nature in this country. With kindest personal regards and invocing [sic] the Lords blessings on yur for yur noble work you are doing for the uplift of humanity.
> Very respectfully yours, Charles Steele, Moran, Texas.

I, personally, think it is very fitting to recall this particular trial now that the magnificent 1883 Shackelford County Courthouse has been totally restored. This trial harks back to those days without overhead projectors, computer generated diagrams, aerial view photographs, and video tape. It recalls a time when oratory could either win or lose a case, the attorney-at-law before the court was the vector and reasoned argument either did or did not carry the day. But, in the spirit of full disclosure, it must also be noted Missouri Matilda Nail Cook's legal fees for all the elegant oratory she received in her defense came to the staggering amount over $14, 000 in 1927 money. Going to court to seek Justice is still a very expensive proposition.

Court House
Albany Tex

1909

8 Restoration Work Summary

by Shirley Caldwell

WHEN THE COUNTY RECEIVED Enhancement Funds from the Texas Department of Transportation (TXDOT) in 1995 for $123,200, everyone was thrilled. At last it meant that Shackelford County could begin the badly needed work on its magnificent stone courthouse. In spite of its exterior elegance, there were real problems there, hidden from the untrained eye but obvious to any good preservationist. The interior looked shabby and dated, really downright embarrassing to those who loved the building, as well as being unsafe because of antiquated heating systems and poor wiring.

The money had been given for the roof—a new copper roof—one that really would last 150 years. When the work began, it became obvious that the clock tower was in bad shape, too, including the cornice. Realizing that it would be much cheaper to do the work while scaffolding was in place, the commissioners led by Judge Montgomery, wisely decided to do all of it at once. The restoration of the clock tower included stripping and painting and the restoration of the four clock-tower windows as well as replacing the historic ridge roll that had been lost over the years.

Architects chosen by TXDOT for the roof work were The Williams Company, AIA, of Austin, Texas, who already had done several courthouse restorations and were doing the Jones County Courthouse which had received enough Enhancement Funds from the highway department to completely restore their building. The first serious dilemma was what color of paint to be used and what to do about the paint on the tower peak. It had been determined that it had probably been painted in the first place because patinas from the copper had streaked the skirting behind the clock faces. After attempting to clean the surfaces and being unsuccessful, it was unanimously decided by the court and advisors present to restore it to the historic image as closely as possible by having paint put on that would leave the impression of the original.

The second problem concerned the four clock-tower windows. They were the original 1884 windows and were in a considerable state of disrepair and deterioration. As the windows were disassembled, it became clear that they could not be saved. The originals were replaced with new ones that exactly matched.

100

Third, the historic ridge roll elements had been lost and modified over the years. The loss of these items considerably compromised the original design and historic detailing of this building. Originally it was decided to reproduce these elements in a phosphatic galvanized material and paint them to match the stone color and the rest of the pressed metal cornice and tower. This idea was discarded in favor of using copper ridge rolls to eliminate the possibility of any chemical action between differing metals. The copper was especially prepared to receive the paint.

The last question to be solved involved the color of paint to use on the tower and pressed metal cornice that was part of the roof project. Lydick-Hooks of Abilene was selected because they were best in installing metal roofs, and they successfully completed the project. Annie Sauser of Restoration Associates Limited performed the paint analysis and using historic photos suggested the proper historic color to use matching the stone color as closely as possible. The result is spectacular!

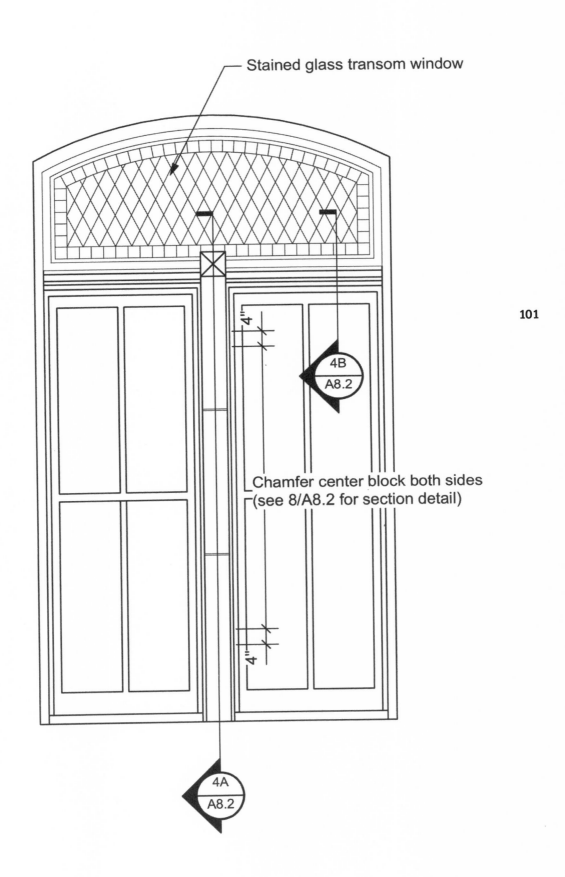

Stained glass transom window

4"

4B
A8.2

Chamfer center block both sides
(see 8/A8.2 for section detail)

4"

4A
A8.2

101

1998

The Texas Historic Courthouse
Preservation Program

by Shirley Caldwell

AS PART OF Texas Governor George W. Bush's re-election campaign in 1998, he boldly announced that part of his platform, in order to save the country's best collection of county buildings, would be the restoration of 220 Texas Historic Courthouses. The preservation community went wild! He asked for $100 million to start the program, and in the end he got $50 million. The Texas Historical Commission received the responsibility of developing and administering the program. After five months of consultations, the Texas Historical Commission announced the program and was astounded when, true to the need they knew was there, more than seventy counties were able to get a master plan ready and indicated they would apply for the money.

On May 4, 2000, in a very dramatic presentation that included cheers and tears, nineteen Texas counties received a total of $42.4 million for their courthouses. Matching grants—85/15—went to Atascosa, Bexar, Donley, Ellis, Erath, Gray, Grimes, Hopkins, Lampasas, Lee, Llano, Maverick, Milam, Presidio, Rains, Red River, Shackelford, Sutton and Wharton counties. Shackelford County received $1,765,440. That the Shackelford County Courthouse made the list is a tribute to the quality of its architecture and its all-around high score. Professional architectural historians were called in to evaluate the buildings in addition to the Historical Commission's professional staff. One outsider who sat in on the evaluation meetings and didn't have her courthouse funded said it was the fairest process she had ever observed. As the winners were announced and their photographs flashed upon a large screen for all to see, it was "as plain as the nose on your face" that the Commission had let the buildings speak for themselves. Everyone who earnestly believes in this program immediately set about to work for the next round of money, the $7.6 million left, and the next appropriation that might be made by the state legislature. With the remaining money, twenty-eight counties were given grants to cover their architectural plans, with the exception of Newton County that got an emergency grant for stabilizing and rebuilding after a tragic fire occurred in August 2000.

104

There are many good reasons why this is a valuable, proactive approach to governing and why our tax dollars are wisely spent in these old buildings, many of which hold a place of honor in the center of their county seat. One of the best reasons is that tourists are fond of these stately county buildings, but citizens realize their value, too. In many counties, the courthouse is architecturally the oldest, grandest building in town. There is an emotional and personal attachment of having marriages, births, and deaths filed in the courthouse. Taxes are paid there, license plates acquired, and court sessions are held. Many are directly connected with elections through registration and early balloting. The courthouse is the most important visible arm of our state in the county. The downright dangerous condition of most of the old courthouses will be eliminated now, and they will be capable of entering a new century with extended, modern capabilities such as wiring to facilitate the computer/fax age and heating/cooling systems that make the buildings habitable during the twenty-first century.

The primary goal of this project is to restore the courthouse exterior to the original appearance and to restore the interior spaces and materials to their 1920s appearance. All proposed work shall include areas below the cornice. Due to funding constraints, only limited site work was included in the project. Commissioners using county equipment handled most of the site work.

The Shackelford County Courthouse received full funding to do essential things. A new access with sloping sidewalk and bridge walkway has been installed at the north entry, in compliance with the Americans for Disabilities Act. An elevator and compliant restrooms were added. All site utilities including water, sewer, and electrical are new. The county provided necessary trenching and back filling. There was new piping installed and draining was improved around the foundation.

The exterior masonry has been cleaned, and inappropriate gray mortar pointing that had been placed on the building in the seventies was removed and replaced with proper mortar and installation. The south fire escape was removed, and the north fire escape repainted. Likewise, the steel windows have been removed and replaced with new wood windows installed to match the original appearance. The window fabrication is in a wood material matching the graining of the interior doors and finished in a dark stain in the interior and a high-quality, waterproof paint on the exterior. Craftsmen restored interior casework to match the interior door detailing per the construction drawings. The four decorative main windows in the district courtroom have matched block and post detail found in the courthouse entry door surrounds. Four new main entry doors have been reconstructed to match original drawing and photographic details.

Demolition included removing the limited amount of asbestos tile and the hallway wall sealing off the south entrance, placed there in the 1930s to provide more county clerk space. Also, the storage closets placed under the stairways and the ladies restroom were removed. Plaster has been applied to duplicate the historic scoring pattern that appears as stone. The existing floors have received a darker stain as has the wainscoting. The beaded board ceiling has been restored and repainted and replaced where necessary. The stairs have been repainted and the baluster reconstructed according to construction drawings. The fifteen offices were restored with refinished floors, painted plaster walls, and restored, replaced, and repainted board ceilings. An elevator, restroom, and utility closet were installed in the northeast quadrant of the first floor by removing a rock safe. The safe door has been retained in its original location. The second floor restroom has been restored with new fixtures and finishes.

The district courtroom has been taken back to its 1920s image, including refinished floors, new skim coated and painted plaster walls and a new decorative metal ceiling. No furniture work was in the general contract.

A new electrical system was a most important addition with a 600 amp service and new main disconnect/meter on a rack system. WTU Electric has installed a new main electrical service transformer and main primary underground service at no cost to the project. The interior electrical service is routed in the crawl space to the new electrical closet. New lighting is in place. Switching and lights on the first and second floors are installed in a concealed manner. For heating and cooling, a new IVAC system included a remote mechanical yard and interior exposed fan coil units in the offices. Air handling units are located in the attic. The plumbing system has been completely replaced with new water/sewer piping.

A series of project meetings were held throughout the restoration process. Project architect was The Williams Company, AIA of Austin, Kim Williams in charge, and the restoration contractor was Phoenix Restoration of Dallas, with Dale Sellers as Project Coordinator and Keith Nichols as Project Manager. The

Shackelford County Commissioner's Court consists of County Judge, Ross Montgomery; Commissioner No. 1, Danny Peacock; Commissioner No. 2, R. P. Mitchell; Commissioner No. 3, Jimmy Brooks; and Commissioner No. 4, Stan West.

The re-dedication of the Shackelford County Courthouse took place on June 30, 2001.

Cheers to Ed Rye and J. E. Flanders! Cheers to the Scottish stone masons! Cheers to Shackelford County!

The Architect's View

by Kim A. Williams, AIA

IN 1995, the Shackelford County Commissioners' Court selected The Williams Company, AIA from a group of several competing architecture firms to guide the Shackelford County Courthouse roof and clocktower restoration. During the course of the project, I, as the county's architect, recommended that they also commission an abbreviated master plan study of the entire courthouse and site. County leadership, under the direction of Judge Ross Montgomery, authorized this additional technical study. Through careful analysis of the courthouse and its site, my staff and I were able to identify many serious problems that were outside the scope of the roof and clocktower restoration.

Timely master planning enabled Shackelford County to establish maintenance and restoration goals and provided counsel for the preservation process. Once the copper roof and metal clocktower restoration was complete in 1997, the county government and I immediately began detailed planning for the correction of the serious electrical, plumbing, and deterioration issues identified in the study.

Coincidentally, Governor George W. Bush had just begun to promote his 1998 reelection initiative to provide major funding for a statewide historic county courthouse preservation program. Bush's funding initiative, which was ultimately brought to life by the Texas Legislature in May

1999, became known as the Texas Historic Courthouse Preservation Program and was placed under the administration of the Texas Historical Commission.

The requirements of the Texas Historic Courthouse Preservation Program mandated a county-funded comprehensive preservation master plan, which The Williams Company, AIA was able to produce quickly and cost effectively based on the previous studies. Thanks to strategic historic research by local citizen Shirley Caldwell and my firm's prompt production of the detailed master plan, the Shackelford County Courthouse was well-positioned to win a grant of $1,765,440 from the Texas Historic Courthouse Preservation Program.

With the grant award in county hands, I immediately began to formulate the most expeditious implementation program that my years of experience could offer. I realized that the slow development of grant program requirements and the turbulence of the construction bidding climate could have a negative impact on a small rural project. As a result, I chose a project delivery method known as "Construction Manager At-Risk" which is rarely used in public projects. My unconventional proposal required the consensus of both the Texas Historical Commission and the State Attorney General's Office.

With the legal groundwork laid, it was now time for the county to choose a construction manager. Recent experience with Phoenix I Restoration and Construction, Ltd., of Dallas led me to wholeheartedly recommend their selection. Dale Sellers, president of Phoenix I, eagerly signed on to serve as construction manager. Thus, the detailed workings of the Construction Manager At-Risk process enabled the formation of a highly qualified team at an extremely competitive price. The total team approach was critical to the success of this challenging historical restoration. Judge Ross Montgomery and the Commissioners Court, the fund-raising committee led by Don Koch, and the staff of the Texas Historical Commission, represented by Dick Ryan and Lyman Labry, were all instrumental in making this restoration effort, the first initiated and completed under the Texas Historic Courthouse Preservation Program, a model for successful project implementation.

Kim Williams, AIA, Principal, and Jason Jennings, Project Manager for The Williams Company, AIA, wish to express the great honor that it has been to take part in the restoration of one of Texas's premier historic structures. Without buildings such as the Shackelford County Courthouse, a vital link to the struggle and determination of our predecessors would be lost. Of course, the success of the project would not have been possible without the help of innumerable dedicated craftspeople. By putting their wide array of talents to use, they helped to return a great Texas building to its former grandeur. It has been a privilege to lead this team of wonderful folks.

110

THE ARCHITECT'S VIEW

Sources

Books and Thesis

Arnold, James R. *Jeff Davis's Own: Cavalry, Comanches, and the Battle for the Texas Frontier.* New York: John Wiley & Sons, 2000.

Blanton, Joseph. *The County Builds a Courthouse.* Albany, Texas: Old Jail Art Foundation, 1983.

Blanton, Joseph Edwin, assisted by Watt Reynolds Matthews. *John Larn.* Albany, Texas: Venture Press, 1994.

Blanton, Thomas Lindsay. *Pictoral Supplement to Interwoven.* Albany, Texas. 1953.

Carter, Robert Goldthwaite. *On the Border With Mackenzie, or Winning West Texas from the Comanches.* Mattituck, New York: J. M. Carroll & Co., 1935.

Cashion, Ty. *A Texas Frontier—The Clear Fork Country and Fort Griffin, 1849-1887.* Norman, Oklahoma: University of Oklahoma Press, 1996.

Dyess, Lt. Colonel William E. *The Dyess Story.* New York: G. P. Putnam, 1944.

Freeman, Martha Doty. *A History of Camp Cooper, Throckmorton County, Texas.* Albany, Texas: Aztec of Albany Foundation, Inc., 1997.

Freeman, Martha Doty. *A History of Fort Phantom Hill, The Post on the Clear Fork of the Brazos River, Jones County, Texas.* Abilene, Texas: Fort Phantom Foundation, 1999.

Holden, William Curry. *Alkali Trails.* Dallas, Texas: The Southwest Press, 1930.

Matthews, Sallie Reynolds. *Interwoven, A Pioneer Chronicle.* Houston, Texas: Anson Jones Press, 1936.

McNair, Sherwyn L. "The Wandering Echo: History of a Frontier Newspaper." M.A. thesis, University of Missouri, 1970.

Metz, Leon Claire. *John Selman—Texas Gunfighter.* Norman, Oklahoma: University of Oklahoma Press, 1966.

Nail, Robert. *A People's Theater.* Albany, Texas: Fort Griffin Fandangle Association, 1970.

The New Handbook of Texas. Vols. 1-6. Austin, Texas: Texas State Historical Association, 1996.

Poe, Sophie A. *Buckboard Days.* Caldwell, Idaho: Caxton Printers, 1936.

Richardson, Rupert N. *The Comanche Barrier to South Plains Settlement.* Glendale, California: The Arthur H. Clark Co., 1933.

Rister, Carl Coke. *Fort Griffin on the Texas Frontier.* Norman, Oklahoma: University of Oklahoma Press, 1956.

Rye, Edgar. *The Quirt and the Spur.* Hammond, Indiana: W. B. Conkey Co., 1909.

Sedwick, John H. *The First Hundred Years—The First National Bank of Albany, Texas*. Albany, Texas: Texas Central Xpress, 1983.

West Texas Historical Association Year Book

Barrett, Arrie. "Western Frontier Forts of Texas." Vol. VII, June, 1931.

Crane, R. C. "Robert E. Lee's Expedition in the Upper Brazos and Colorado County." Vol. XIII, October, 1937.

Crimmins, Colonel M. L. "Camp Cooper and Fort Griffin, Texas." Vol. XVII, October, 1941.

Farmer, Mrs. L. E. "Fort Davis on the Clear Fork of the Brazos." Vol. XXXIII, October, 1957.

Grant, Ben O. "Citizens Law Enforcement Bodies: A Little More About the Vigilantes." Vol. XXXIX, October, 1963.

Grant, Ben O., and J. R. Webb, "On the Cattle Trail and Buffalo Range." Vol. XI, November 1935.

Hammons, Anne. "West Texas Delegates to the State Constitutional Convention of 1875." Vol. XII, July, 1936.

Haskew, Eula. "Stribling and Kirkland of Fort Griffin." Vol. XXXII, October, 1956.

Howarth, Jacob. "Letter, Experiences of an Ex-Soldier." Vol. II, June, 1926.

Hutto, John R. "Mrs. Elizabeth (Aunt Hank) Smith." Vol. XV, October, 1939.

Marchman, Watt P., and Robert C. Cotner. "Indian Agent Jesse Stem: A Manuscript Revelation." Vol. XXXIX, October, 1963.

Webb, J. R. "Henry Herron, Pioneer and Peace Officer During Fort Griffin Days." Vol. XX, October, 1944.

Court Documents

Commissioners Court Minutes, County Clerk Office, Shackelford County Courthouse, Albany, Vols. 1, 2, 3, 4, 5, 6, 7, 8, 9, 10, 17.

County Court Minutes, County Clerk Office, Shackelford County Courthouse, Albany, Vol. 1.

District Court Minutes, County Clerk Office, Shackelford County Courthouse, Book B, 259th District Court Records—Ray Seedig File.

Deed of Trust Records, County Clerk Office, Shackelford County Courthouse, Vol. 10.

Deed of Trust Records, County Clerk Office, Shackelford County Courthouse, Index, Vol. G2.

Newspapers

The Abilene Reporter News, 1956, 1958, 1965.

The Albany Echo, 1882, 1883, 1884.

The Albany News, 1884, 1887, 1903, 1905, 1921, 1922, 1935, 1940, 1943, 1947, 1948, 1964, 1974, 1976, 1985.

The Albany Star, 1883.

The Breckenridge American, 1976.

Official Texas Historical Marker Narratives

Brooks, Audrey. "Cottle No. 1—First Commercial Gas Well West of Corsicana, Texas." Caldwell File, Albany, 1974.

Green, Robert, and Shirley Caldwell. "Henry Carter Jacobs House." Caldwell File, Albany, 1974.

Green, Robert, and Shirley Caldwell, "The Texas Central Railway Co." Caldwell File, Albany, 1975.

Moore, Vaughan, Marilynne Jacobs, and Shirley Caldwell. "The Cook Ranch Field." Caldwell File, Albany, 1976.

"Moran—The Town That Has Had Three Names." Caldwell File, 1975.

Turner, Mrs. Elsa McFarland. "Shackelford County." 1975.

Robert Nail Archives, Old Jail Art Center, Albany: Joseph Blanton Collection; Webb Collection; Newspaper Collection; Robert Nail Photograph Collection; A. A. Clarke Papers

Index

Bill Cauble

116

117

119

Van Jones